D1342766

Changing
Youth
Worship

Changing
Youth
Worship

Patrick Angier

NATIONAL SOCIETY/CHURCH HOUSE PUBLISHING

National Society/Church House Publishing,
Church House,
Great Smith Street,
London SW1P 3NZ

ISBN 0 7151 4892 3

Published 1997 by the National Society/Church House Publishing

Acknowledgement

Brenda LeFave, 'I need you to hold me' (p. 47) is copyright © Mercy/Vineyard Publishing/Music Services, administered by Copycare, P.O. Box 77, Hailsham BN27 3EF, UK. Used by permission.

Cover design by Sarah Hopper

Printed in England by Biddles Ltd, Guildford and King's Lynn

Contents

List of useful terms

Alternative worship Used to describe the expression of faith that grows out of a new faith community as it seeks authentic spiritual engagement within and representation through its own post-modern culture.

Bricolage Improvised creativity in which objects and expressions are used in ways that alter or subvert their original purpose or meaning.

Charismata The gifts of the Holy Spirit.

Contemporary worship Describes the wide range of worship styles, using hymns and choruses, preaching, drama, dance, music group etc., that are the mainstay of many churches. It is worship that does not necessarily need sacred space but comfortable space.

Culture-specific worship That worship which is produced by, with and for a particular culture, sub-culture or group. This may take the form of a culture-specific service or a culture-specific congregation, depending on the structures and organization of the group.

Detatched work Youth work that is not club based but which takes place through the development of relationships with young people where they hang out, on the streets, in the park, etc.

Enculturing The process of removing one set of cultural values and codes from something and expressing it through a different culture's set of values and codes.

Macro-culture The structure or canvas of societal values, world-views and perceptions on and in which popular culture, art, fashion etc., operate.

Micro-culture Those aspects of fashion, taste, artistic expression and popular culture which are transitory. Changes within the micro-cultural framework are arbitrary.

Missioning Reaching out to people to engage them with the

Christian message in holistic and culturally appropriate ways.

Modernism Describes the cultural world view that developed after the Renaissance and through the Age of Enlightenment, characterized by the rise of institutional structures in Church, industry, state, etc. and the idea of progress.

New Churches Describes those worshipping communities which were formerly called House Churches and, although non-denominational, are part of mainstream Christianity.

New Faith Communities Groups of Christians still exploring what it means to be Christian and the Church in their situation or culture without having settled for a particular ecclesiological emphasis.

Popular culture This term not only describes those areas of culture that are popular, e.g. music, magazines, television, etc. It also describes the 'sphere of exchange, interpretation and conflict between different social groups.' (Open University U203, *Concepts Glossary*, 1983, p.12)

Post-modernism Describes that which is following the break-down of the unifying strands of modernism, characterized by fragmentation, networking and non-institutional cultural forms, beginning in architecture, art and literature and spreading more widely through popular culture. Post-modernity offers both challenge and opportunity to the Church.

Prospective worship A term used to describe the form that worship will take twenty years from now. The proto-forms of prospective worship are happening today but as yet we do not know which, if any, will become the dominant ones.

Rites, the rite The combination of liturgy and action to explain and make accessible spiritual realities.

Traditional worship Worship that draws on the historic liturgies, music and resources of the Church and rejects the copying of contemporary culture.

Introduction

The last few years have seen an explosion of creativity in the realm of youth worship. There has been the rise of new worship, radical worship, Celtic worship, culturally-relevant worship, rave worship, sanctified dance and alternative worship, to name just a selection. This explosion has not gone unnoticed both within the Church and outside. Articles have appeared in *Mixmag*,[1] *Monocle*, *Youthwork*, *Young People Now* and local and national newspapers, as well as in the church press. Discussion on the Internet and features on Radios 1 and 4, and TV (*God in the House*, the recent Channel 4 series) have increased the awareness of this kind of worship. This has provided a framework for questions to be asked and heightened people's hopes or anxieties about this issue. Forms of youth worship have sent shock waves through the Church at every level as their sphere of activity has increased. In the Church of England the influence of these alternatives has swept through diocesan and deanery initiatives, been present in deanery restructuring plans, parochial church council discussions and parish worship experiments. Whereas once they were rare, now these alterations have become a commonplace feature of the modern Church.

This explosion of activity and interest is not just limited to Anglican experience; it crosses denominational barriers and challenges the very structures of all Churches and traditions. Each new situation is different and unique, fuelling discussion and debate over how local churches and congregations should respond to the new issues and problems that confront them.

- How does an ecumenical youth congregation, originally launched by the local churches, feed back into the sponsoring Churches?

- What happens if those best able to support an Anglican youth church plant belong to one of the 'New Church' networks – do we get protective or do we become flexible?

● Can such things as youth churches/congregations be a valid expression of Christianity anyway?

These are examples of the questions challenging many mainstream congregations and churches today; hard questions which demand honesty, vision and respect. The questions which these issues force us to ask will take us on a journey which challenges both our theology of the Church and our theology of worship, and demands that we take a fresh look at what it means to be worshipping congregations approaching the year 2000.

Is youth worship just a new expression of worship, a passing style or something radically different and permanent?

What are the catalysts or causes of its evolution? Is it a single phenomenon or are we seeing the consequences of a series of influences coming together?

Different combinations of these influences affecting different people and situations produce different forms of worship; the result is the wide range of developments that have been appearing all over Britain. The researchers for the *God in the House* TV series visited over a hundred services and events and received videotapes from a further eighty.

Are these something to be welcomed as the panacea for all the Church's ills, a harmless distraction that will never really change anything, or a dangerous blind alley which already, with the collapse of Sheffield's Nine O'clock Service (NOS), has caused irreparable hurt and lasting damage?

This book explores some of the issues surrounding the phenomenon of youth worship. It draws on my experience as a youth minister involved in the 1980s and early 1990s in youth worship and the development of what was later labelled an 'alternative' worship service. During this period new styles of worship were evolving independently in many places around the country from the grass-roots up.

In addition to exploring these forms of worship, this book tries to identify the causes and influences that have given rise to this grass-roots movement and the different emphases within it.

The two most common questions I am asked about youth congregations are 'Is it right to have a separate youth congregation?' in the light of the Bible's teaching on the Church as neither Jew nor Greek, slave nor free etc.? and 'What happens when a youth congregation grows up?' These questions are addressed in the later chapters, along with guidelines on good practice for doing worship and getting started.

This book is not an encyclopaedia of the alternative worship scene, with great lists of who is doing what and where, when they started and how each practitioner compares; nor is it a resource anthology with a thousand and one ideas for alternative worship. This book tries to provide a framework for those who want to know more about what is happening and why. It suggests a way of categorizing and exploring the developments in the youth worship scene and offers a format by which we can all positively evaluate the form. It will also give help and guidance to those wishing to start or develop ways of being the Church that are more culturally friendly to groups that do not feel at home in a traditional church.

This book does not, and cannot, explore all the options, answer all the questions or give unlimited insight on every situation. I hope that it will act as a catalyst for further reflection on not only a Christian understanding of culture and meaning, but also the theology of the continuing nature of worship and the Church.

1

Something is happening in youth worship

> The primary frontier which needs to be crossed in mission to young people is not so much a generation gap as a profound change in the overall culture. Todays young people will have to find ways of discipleship which are not familiar to adults in the Church. Not all that older generations attempt to pass on will be helpful.[1]

There are many starting points for exploring the relationship between worship and young people. It is an issue much in view and much in vogue at the moment and we all approach the subject with our own experiences, expectations, hopes and anxieties. Even the phrase 'youth worship' conjures up many different images.

Are we talking about images of yesteryear with a few teenagers gathered around a guitar, or yester-decade with rows of teenagers dressed in white walking up for confirmation? Are we thinking of large events like Greenbelt or Spring Harvest, Iona or Taizé? Is our experience one of churches with ageing congregations, few or no young people and feelings of guilt, failure and a sort of bleak hopelessness for the future? Or have we experienced or heard of something new described as alternative worship, experimental worship, or youth church, where Christian young people are growing in numbers and commitment? Is there also an element of doubt? Is it really church? Is it really worship? What happens when they grow up? This is a subject which is very difficult to approach objectively and we therefore find it easier to assign blame for the things we do not like or quite understand than to spend time looking at the roots of what is happening and commend what is valuable.

Cultural change

My starting point is to look at the cultural change that is taking place as we reach the end of the twentieth century. This is not simply the micro-cultural change of tastes and preferences that happens alongside every change of generation and causes every parent to yell, 'Turn that row down!' to their kids' music. (*Micro-culture* is the term used to describe the mixture of arts, popular arts and popular culture that changes with fashion and passing generations.) Rather, we are seeing a macro-cultural change from modernism to post-modernism. These changes affect not only the style and form of things but also the major foundational meanings and perception frameworks within which we operate.

Macro-culture is the overall structure within which micro-culture is expressed. Changes in macro-culture are different from those in micro-culture. Changes in micro-culture make things unfashionable; changes in the macro-culture make things irrelevant.

All too often, as the Church, we are left arguing heatedly over the micro-cultural issues, thinking we are being 'with it', without realizing that all we are doing is demonstrating our own irrelevance.

This macro-cultural change is part of the reason why the Church is failing to have an impact not only upon teenagers but also young adults. The *Coventry Diocesan Directory* states:

> The Church of England in Warwickshire and the City of Coventry has probably no more than 150 young people each year who pass the age of eighteen and remain in its regular worshipping life. Furthermore, it is estimated that most of these have at least one parent who attends church. Probably no more than a dozen young people a year reach adult status having come to faith from an unchurched background.[2]

The situation in this diocese is probably no different from that in many others. Young people have been and are constantly drifting away from the worshipping life of the Church and its youth organizations. How do we respond to this decline? Do we batten down the hatches, create our own Christian subculture and try to protect our children and young people from the evil culture out there? This is an almost instinctive response. However, it is a response which puts us firmly on the road to further decline and the marginalization of Christianity in this country.

In contrast some people have responded by engaging with the culture, finding out what is happening and why, meeting young people on their territory, using their terms, and enculturing both the message and the expression of the message into youth culture.

This profound change in culture and the enculturation of new forms is crucial in much that is happening in the realm of worship. Have you ever seen those missionary photographs taken earlier this century, the sort that live in the dark recesses of the Sunday school cupboard and show African Christians dressed up in Western choir robes, or Western-style suits, singing Western hymns or listening to white, Western clergy? They are evidence of a complete, if well-intentioned, disregard for any aspects of indigenous culture. Today life is very different: the indigenous Churches of Africa, Latin America and China show rapid growth; they have their own ministers, training methods, music, liturgical traditions etc. Today, if we were making our first missionary trips to a group of unreached people we would try not to repeat the mistakes that were made in the eighteenth and nineteenth centuries – or would we? Young people can be seen as just such a group of unreached people and the Church could be in danger of making the same mistakes as in its imperial past.

Culture and popular culture in our society today are more fragmented than at any other time in history. The number of unifying strands are constantly diminishing, while the range of choices continually increases in terms of style and form. This has meant the emergence of a plethora of subcultures. So to talk of 'youth worship' suddenly requires a different language, a broad perspective and particular definitions.

We now have a youth culture that could be called 'pre-non-Christian'. As Bob Mayo says,

They identified a group of street kids hanging around the street corner, where the church stood, as not 'non christian', but pre-non christian. To be a Christian involves choice. You cannot make that choice if you know nothing of the options.[3]

Many young people are more than three generations away from the Church. Their parents and grandparents did not go and still do not go to church. Their schools have only taught a pale reflection of real Christianity. Religious television, as they see it, only has a fair smattering of religious nutters, perverts or sad cases in its programmes. Where is accurate information going to come from?

Youth culture is so diverse and estranged from church culture that traditional attempts at socializing young people into church culture will in the main be ineffective.[4] This socializing has been a longstanding process whereby from childhood up through youth group children are taught the norms, roles and behaviour patterns of their faith. This traditional method, based upon relationships within the congregation and home, is already breaking down under the weight of cultural changes as large numbers of teenagers drop out of church life and faith. For those young people who have no contact with the Church, it is an equally ineffective method of producing mature Christians. Young people who have not learned that you do not light up a cigarette as the vicar starts his sermon (as one young person did on his first visit to morning worship) need both active and relevant forms of discipleship to develop a lasting faith and also in many cases different styles of worship. A flippant and amusing example, but it must challenge us to think and not judge.

This culture gap is far-reaching and ever-increasing. The Church is faced with the task of finding a new way of connecting and missioning our young people within a multi-faceted and ever-changing youth culture. Rather as a monk arriving in a community a thousand years ago might have explored what was going on, met needs and lived alongside the people, missioning is more than evangelism, more than socialization, more than

8

identification – it is about incarnation, a concept that is now often over-used but still very important. We must find new ways to get alongside people where they are and make God real for them. For some, this will mean hanging out on the streets with detached work; for others it will be mobilizing and equipping young people to reach their friends and peers; for others, running counselling and advice centres or sailing holidays, or teaching driving skills and car maintenance. There are a multitude of ways of either working outside the Church to bring youth culture in, or inside the Church to take its culture out. Missioning can be about starting things from nowhere or building on things that are already there. There is no one set pattern. The day when one style of youth ministry fitted all has long gone. We need to find out what God wants us to do to share in his mission here and now.

Changing worship

Much that is happening in the Church today in terms of worship comes as a direct result of its different mission approaches to the prevailing culture. None of these expressions of worship should be looked at in isolation; there is an interchange and cross-fertilization of ideas, resources and technology that results in a breaking down of traditional labels and terms. For the sake of convenience these types of mission approach may be seen as loosely falling into patterns. We shall be looking at these patterns in more detail later, but these different approaches help us to see from the outset that similar things may be happening in youth worship, in terms of both style and content, but for very different reasons.

Planting out In this approach, church plants are made into the external youth culture. Christian groups identify unreached groups or subcultures within an area, identify the cultural characteristics of that group and reach out to it in cross-cultural mission. At first most of the leadership and team will be from the parent group, enculturing faith to the subculture; but as the plant takes root indigenous members and leadership will develop. In church-planting language, this would be a plant into an 'unreached peoples group'. Examples of Churches that fit this category would include Bliss, XTC (now ended) and many of the youth churches associated with Remix.

Growing out Here the church grows out of the external youth culture. Christian youth workers, working alongside young people who are outside the Church, in detached work, coffee-bar ministry or schools, develop relationships with groups of young people. After making a Christian commitment the young people move on to express their worship of God in culturally relevant forms. At first this may be in a small group or in experimental worship but over time a service and congregation will gradually grow and reach beyond the initial people contacted to the cultural peers of the members. Examples of this type of church/congregation are The Gap (which grew out of work in schools) or Joy (a product of detached work).

Growing in The internal youth-grown congregation is the most common type of youth worship and in church-planting language would be a 'preference plant', except that in this instance few evolve into separate churches. Young people within the life of the Church, engaging with the culture outside, develop worship styles that can reach their friends outside the Church and reflect their own culture. Often these have a strong emphasis on participation and consequently there is a strong sense of ownership by the young people. These can be weekly youth congregations, or monthly or occasional services. This group would include Holy Disorder, Agape, Lifetime, The Gig and many others.

Planting in Internal congregation multiplication by culture. The gap between cultures within the Church is such that it often becomes mutually beneficial to multiply congregations along cultural lines. A smaller group moves out from the mainstream to establish a more authentic act of worship at a different time and sometimes at a different venue. The new congregation could evolve into a separate church but may not necessarily do so. This grouping would include Be Real, the NOS and the Late Late Service.

Bridge events These are not congregations or churches but mission outreach into youth culture. Containing a mixture of worship and entertainment, they provide a place for Christians to bring their non-Christian friends, ideas and resources to incorporate into worship within congregations and can also be the launching pad for church planting. Examples of such outreaches include the Warehouse, Awesome and Rave in the Nave.

It is also important to note another category of worship experiment which is not a mission approach: the imitation of something else. I once visited a church that had five teenagers, where the vicar said, 'We want to do alternative worship to get the young people in.' No one had consulted with the young people to find out what would be an authentic form of worship for them, their friends or the wider youth culture. Putting coloured lights, video screens and candles into a service does not in itself make it culturally relevant. Nor are style and formation process the only characteristics that help define what is happening; theology, power structure and authenticity are equally important.

Defining terms

ALTERNATIVE WORSHIP

This is probably a good point at which to pause and define some of the terms used in this book. One of the most prominent difficulties concerning youth worship is that of language: different groups use words to mean different things. 'Alternative worship' and 'the alternative worship scene' are phrases often used in an all-embracing fashion to describe what is happening. It is a convenient expression for the national church press and media to use. *Youth A Part* states:

> It is a phenomenon which almost invites misunderstanding. It is not a youth service or experimental worship or Rave in the Nave or an evangelistic campaign. Those involved in this have been frustrated at the attempts to place this into one of the Church's pre-existing

11

categories. At some point (it is suggested this may have been Greenbelt 1991) some people began to refer to alternative worship.[5]

Alternative worship as a label is not without its own problems. In the past there have been alternative theatre, alternative comedy, alternative lifestyles and alternative energy sources. These are all alternatives to an existing mainstream form. Alternative worship, if it is just the alternative to the existing mainstream form, could include anything from rave to Taizé, Celtic to charismatic, depending on the type of mainstream service.

Some see alternative worship as doing something alternative to worship, and therefore not worship. For others it is a label to attach to whatever they are doing, or even retrospectively to what they were doing, in order to gain 'street cred' and recognition. Despite the reservations, alternative worship is an accurate description of some of the new things that are happening in worship in some areas, but it is not an all-embracing term. In this book, alternative worship is used to describe a type of worship that in most cases

- is post-modern in emphasis;
- does not embrace traditional or contemporary worship;
- has a leadership which is not hierarchical but democratic;
- is exploratory in its theology and develops new rituals;
- is not done by the Church for others.

Alternative worship is the expressed form of faith that grows out of a new faith community as it seeks authentic spiritual engagement within and 'representation' through its own post-modern culture.

If this description defines alternative worship, we still need to find a way to describe the broader developments and the scene beyond the specific.

CULTURALLY-RELEVANT WORSHIP VS ALTERNATIVE WORSHIP

Some groups prefer to talk of culturally-relevant worship and this has a number of advantages:

- Many of the groups involved are concerned with being relevant to those who find the gap between their culture and church culture too wide to cross.

- The Christian gospel at the core is not altered, only the worship that expresses that gospel.

- Jesus' incarnation was about God coming and living in a particular time, place and culture and being relevant to it.

There are, however, a number of problems with it as a label:

- If something is culturally relevant, then other things are by definition culturally irrelevant. This is a subjective judgement at best and at worst quite insulting to those who have worshipped faithfully in a particular style.

- There is a danger of associating cultural relevance with spiritual relevance; the two are far from synonymous.

- It is a transient definition. If culture changes so does what is culturally relevant, otherwise it ceases to be relevant.

In the light of this, instead of defining what is happening in terms of cultural relevance, we can do so in terms of 'culture specificity'.

CULTURE-SPECIFIC WORSHIP

Culture-specific worship describes worship produced by, with or for a particular culture. A culture-specific congregation is drawn from or worships within a particular culture.

Definitions using 'culture-specific' have a number of advantages. They enable us to place what is happening into a wider context. Over the 300 years between the Prayer Book and Series One, everyone was expected to worship in the same way. Culture was not an issue within the Anglican Church; wherever you went you would use the same prayer book, the same lectionary readings etc. This would also have been true of the Latin Mass for Roman Catholics worldwide up to the Second Vatican Council. Over the last 30 years we have seen a shift away from what I shall term 'culturally non-specific worship' ('one size fits all') towards more culturally-specific forms of worship. The Alternative

Service Book provides just that – alternative forms of service – and *Church Family Worship* and *Patterns for Worship* have taken this a step further with their pick-and-mix approach to liturgy. The need to relate to people where they are is being recognized along with the differences between age groups, areas and cultural groups.

Besides using this definition to describe what is happening in worship with young people and in post-modern expressions of the Church, we can also use it to embrace what is happening in the wider Church. In the realm of church-planting there are a range of culture-specific congregations originating in deaf culture, black culture, Asian culture or student culture. In *Faith in the City* and other church reports we see the need to enculture the faith for specific communities in ways that are still not possible using our present liturgy.

'Youth worship', 'alternative worship', 'rave worship' and church plants into youth culture are part of a larger process of enculturation of the gospel for differing communities that can be described as culture-specific worship.

Experiencing worship

Before we look in detail at this process of enculturation, let us take a whistle-stop tour around some of the experiences which we might come across in the world of young people and worship. It is not easy to put on to paper something that is both highly visual and experiential, but I will try to give you a taste of the flavour. With several hundred youth churches, youth congregations and alternative worship services to choose from, here are a few samples of the range of services, events and gatherings that you might encounter within the wide range of culture-specific worship events. For each I have tried to draw out a few of the key, striking features without burying it in too much descriptive detail. Let us start on a warm spring Sunday evening in Norwich.

THE NIGHT-CLUB

It is a Sunday night. The queue for the night-club runs fifty yards up the road. Inside, the music is pumped up and the atmosphere is close with perspiration as 400 young people hit the dance floor. The full effect of the club's light-show cuts the air. This is no poor church-hall imitation, this is Norwich Youth For Christ's Supernova.

The music varies from current dance music, chart sounds to leading Christian bands. The video screen flashes up images, pictures, information and song lyrics (it's not only the Christian ones that have good words). No drink or drugs here, it's a safe place to be.

Everyone is jumpin' in the house of God . . . but is it worship? There are moments in Bon Jovi's 'Livin' on a Prayer', as the MC cuts the sound and everyone sings together, and also in some World Wide Message Tribe songs, when we can see the sort of unity that comes in corporate worship. But, equally, might it not be the unity of the football terraces? Is the information from the video screens any less effective as a means of communication than a sermon? Is finding one of the team to talk to all that different from the church ministry team or pastoral visitors? Supernova is on the edge because of its clientele: half the young people here are pre-non-Christian; others are on the outer fringes of church youth groups but would never go near a church. It is also on the edge because it stands on the boundary between straightforward entertainment which is therefore fairly 'safe' and something with a spiritual dynamic. Non-church young people would class it as religious, not in a negative way but because it has a 'spirituality'. Church young people cannot make the same classification. There is something different about the quality of its 'religiosity'. 'The atmosphere is Electric better than Church.'[6]

15

THE EVENT

Doughnuts and non-alcoholic cocktails by the organ; bouncy castles in the north aisle. Prayer zone underneath the tower. If you want to chill-out, the hippy house is in the Lady Chapel. George arrives in five minutes, so get ready for the welcome.

Nearly 800 young people have gathered for Awesome (but it could be Dragonfly, Rave in the Nave, M7 or any one of many other youth events). The fast-moving action cuts between stages: worship on one and band/competition/games on another. Hi-tech lights, multiple video screens and effects transform the vast empty church. The whole event is a eucharist (literally, thanksgiving); after an opening confession with candles of forgiveness and inclusive up-tempo worship, there is time to bounce on a bouncy castle, tie a prayer knot, relax with boot painting and friendship bracelets in the hippy house or listen to the band's opening set before getting back to the worship area to hear the Archbishop being interviewed by a young person. As the evening reaches the consecration and distribution, the focus becomes obvious: light and sound draw people to the act of communion itself, before an explosion of praise and celebration sends them out to live and work to God's praise and glory.

THE YOUTH SERVICE

The church is in almost complete darkness except for a faint red glow lighting the pews. Shadowy banners hang from beams and the hiss of the PA system is lost in the hushed murmurings of the congregation of about 90, most of them young people. The hiss of the PA grows to a deafening roar of helicopter engines as we are taken on a breathtaking ride through God's creation on a giant video screen.

The picture freezes on a beautiful sunrise over mountains and trees. 'God created us beautiful, unique and special,' announces the leader, 'but this has happened.' Taking up a stick, she strikes the video projector screen. It's made of paper and rips and tears, shattering and distorting the image as the paper screen fragments flap. 'God's image, the way he made us.' The piece of paper is ripped up, divided and used to write on during the confession. After the confession, the songs are familiar, often well known but arranged to a dance beat and pre-recorded. There is a lot of youth input: young people lead the songs and the linking Bible passages and operate the lights, smoke machine, PA and other technical stuff. The talky bit is interspersed with two video clips (the paper screen now replaced by the real one) and a drama sketch. The prayers are in small groups with visual reminders for prayer in word and picture projected on to the screen.

Afterwards, the eight hours of setting up are reversed in a quarter of the time. The service is very recognizable: confession, praise, Bible reading, sermon and prayers, but the method, style, atmosphere and congregation are very different.

THE ALTERNATIVE

There are about 25 people present, most of them in their late 20s and 30s but one or two are older. The space is open, a triangular shape between three large hanging banners, two with slide images and one used later for chant lyrics. There are a few simple coloured lights, lots of candles and burning incense sticks. We use a Celtic confession, backed by the steady rhythms that ebb and flow through the service, drawing us into song and reflection. The mix of male and female voices leading from among us adds to the strong sense of togetherness. Pearls of wisdom are distributed, held tight, shared as we are led through a gentle reflective time of teaching. The songs have that same Celtic feel despite the dance beat and very English setting. All too quickly it is over; the service has lasted some forty minutes but then it is time to descend for hot home-made soup, bread and cheese, bottles of wine and togetherness.

THE YOUTH CONGREGATION

The school hall stage is empty, with the band positioned on the floor half-way down one side next to a large screen for video and song lyrics. A few coloured lights illuminate the band and the semicircles of chairs are well spaced, with plenty of room in the aisles.

There are usually about sixty in the congregation but with two youth groups visiting tonight the numbers are swollen to over a hundred. The service begins with a time of sung worship: praise moving into adoration, interspersed by a reading from Scripture, a stillness in the spirit where the gentle sound of singing in tongues flows over the congregation. After the sung worship there are notices, testimony, a single song and then the talky bit. It's twenty minutes long but the young people are attentive as the leader in his twenties expounds Joshua.

After the talk it's prayer in twos and threes, with themes shown on the screen. Then it's back to praise with the latest Matt Redman and Martin Smith numbers and an opportunity to respond or receive ministry while others grab a coffee or soft drink. The two hours have flown by and as I head for the car I hear one of the visiting youth leaders trying to explain to her youth group why morning service at their church could not be like this instead of the boring . . .

These are just a few snapshots of what is happening. We could have also mentioned cell churches, rave worship services, modern rituals, and many more. One of the great strengths of culture-specific worship is that it is different from place to place and community to community. Not only does culture/specific worship vary from community to community, but it is also constantly changing and evolving within the community as new technological skills are learnt and experimented with, new rituals are developed and those involved grow and change spiritually.

If we return to our definition of culture-specific worship as worship developed by, with or for a particular culture, we can see how our snapshots can all be fitted into this definition. They may all be broadly within youth culture but they meet the spiritual needs of very different sub-groups within that culture. Some young people would feel just as uncomfortable, perhaps even more so, within a culture-specific worship event that was not specific to their subculture.

I visited one event where the post-modern style of worship completely failed to engage the young people and they went off to take advantage of other options at the event. At another event the opportunity for the worship band to lead an extended time of charismatic praise songs was the time for the vast majority to depart for home. I say this not in blame or judgement, because both worship times were holy, well planned and well put together, and in the right context would have been great. However, we need to be wary of trying to transplant culture-specific worship from one context to another without going back to first principles.

2

Dry ice and laser beams

Isaac Watts would have fallen out of his organ loft, John Wesley would have dropped his hymn book but to the youngsters at St. Stephen's dry ice and laser beams are where it is at . . . out are sermons and hymns, in are rock music, disco lighting, overhead projectors, microphones and workshop chats on the issues of the day . . . it takes all day to transform the 1841 church into something that resembles a night-club, banners proclaiming the faith are strung up round the beams of the open-timbered church. The pulpit is removed and a stage of electrical musical instruments is set up . . . by 8 p.m. the church is purposely almost dark. Young people can just wander in and find a place. After an informal welcome the interior of the building is ablaze with colour and echoing to the beat of pop music.[1]

Flashing lights, smoke machines, live music group. These are the things that a lot of people would notice when entering a Holy Disorder service but there is a whole lot more . . . within the service we would also have workshops such as drama, meditations, art, dance etc. These workshops would give each person a chance to get to know each other and explore a theme.[2]

In the previous chapter we had a brief look at some of the range of things that are happening in culture-specific worship. In this chapter we are going to look at this in more detail. So after the shock of metaphorically walking into either of the above services, what do you experience, how is it different, what touches the senses and what lifts the spirit?

> On the first visit to a service, the main impression is visual. Screens and hanging fabrics, containing a multiplicity of colours moving and static images continuously dominate the perceptions.[3]

Is this high visual content the only difference between culture-specific worship and more mainstream services, or are there other areas of difference or surprising areas of common ground that we should note?

Worship ingredients

The difference is not just restricted to the externals of music, style, technology and imagery. It is also present in the process of planning and putting on worship, as well as in group structures and theology. We may find that culture-specific worship is not just worship with modern songs, but something of a radically different nature. But is it? As we look at some of the more practical aspects of culture-specific worship, we shall find that the core purpose of its activities has a similar base to the activities in a mainstream church. It could be an expression of praise or a means of focusing on an activity. In the days when the Mass was said in Latin, a bell was rung at the holy bit so that people knew when it was happening. Some churches still use the practice today. In a culture-specific worship service a back-projected image of Christ on the cross might be used at a similar stage in the proceedings, on a large white screen behind the altar. Rituals such as the washing of feet in the Maundy Thursday service[4] or the giving of a grape to someone at Spring Harvest to represent forgiveness all help people to understand the meaning and significance of something spiritual by using a practical picture. Culture-specific worship rituals, be they flames, feathers or fireworks, are there to serve the same purpose.

We need to look next in more detail at how the visual, ritualistic and liturgical content of the rite is put together. The powerful visual impression made in this kind of worship is constructed from a variety of ingredients, not just the use of video images; the whole effect comes from how the whole space is set up. For example, hanging banners can be screens for projected slide images or intelligent lighting. They can be painted with graphics, messages or declarations of faith, be blank except when ultraviolet lights shine on them, or act as backdrops and curtains to change and shape the space, in addition to their simple use as screens for video or OHP images.

LIGHTING

Lighting is another ingredient which not only differs in complexity and cost but can also be used in a variety of ways. One of the questions we need to consider, concerning the semiotics of lighting, is: What are the 'encoded' messages we are conveying in our use of lighting? Does focusing all our lighting on 'the stage' with the worship group, for example, convey the unspoken message that this is just the Christian equivalent of a rock concert and that worship is a spectator sport in which we only participate when we sing along with the songs?

Can lighting be used in different ways to convey different messages? Lighting the worship space itself with colours and effects can be part of a total visual image that not only evokes mood and atmosphere with colour, pattern, style and movement but may also advance the narrative of our worship and move the liturgy on in the same way that the liturgical action in a traditional church service moves from one place to another depending on the activity. The use of a simple change in colour can be just such a signifier, as can the use of ultraviolet or pinspots on a rotating mirror-ball. Lighting does not have to be complicated or expensive; having done both large- and small-scale worship events, I know that low-key and sometimes low-tech can play as important a part as the more hi-tech styles.

VISUALS

Video, slide and film-loop imagery on back or front projector screens, banners and multiple TV screens are integral ingredients in many of the services, but not all. Their use can vary from illustrations to teaching to aids during prayer, as the Bishop of Wakefield, Nigel McCulloch, reflected after a visit to an alternative worship service in Huddersfield:

> I was struck by the high visual content, There was good use of multi videos, especially as a commentary on the scriptures – showing poverty in Africa and war scenes to accompany verses about God's love and care. It took us into another plane, very different from my normal experience of worship – far beyond the music, words, architecture and movement or even the more imaginative mainstream worship. It clearly helped the young people to worship.

Elsewhere there is a post-modern form of expression with an apparently chaotic bombardment of visual images, a 'bricolage of signs' from which the worshippers can draw their own meanings and interpretations.

> The 45-minute service had no preaching, hymns or organized prayers. Instead, it was set out like a Celtic Labyrinth. People walked through the first part dropping their troubles as they did and came to the centre – a white room lit by ultraviolet light and fuelled with ambient music. Here was a time of contemplation before the walk out, where, amidst house music, videos of priests breaking bread to sonic booms and phrases such as 'eat God' flashing up, you walk out, opening yourself to God. It was, in the words of several who attended, 'better than any club'.[5]

Between these two positions there are a multiple number of ways in which moving images can be used to engage us liturgically, raise our perceptions, challenge our understandings and illuminate our spirits, as the Archbishop of Canterbury wrote on his pilgrimage to Taizé:

> When young people start to experiment with worship they will need to use symbols. Some they will bring from

their own culture. But on hand is the language of symbols, sacraments and signs which the Christian faith supplies in abundance and which can be adapted to their culture . . . much more could be done by older Christians in exploring the imagery which young people employ to make sense of the world around them. We sometimes fail young people by our lack of imagination.[6]

SHAPING THE SPACE

Lighting, screens, projected images and 'the bank of electronic instruments' are all part of the construction and creation of the worship space but not the entirety. Many more aspects need to be considered when setting up, in order to create a feel that will be complementary to the worship experience. What is the shape of the space? Can people move around? Are there pews, chairs or beanbags? Is there one focus or several? Do those responsible for leading do so from up front or from within the congregation, from one place or many? How are other artistic forms used? Is there a role for icons?

The answers to these questions give each act of worship and culture-specific congregation a uniqueness even before we bring the action into our space. One word of caution: 'As the ancients warned us, whatever is poured in a glass – be it champagne or dishwater – will take the shape of the container and be limited by its capacity.'[7]

MUSIC

The style of music varies dramatically from service to service. For some it is an opportunity to use the more upbeat contemporary choruses that are too lively for the main services. For others it is an occasion for lengthy times of sung worship. And for yet others the rock beat of contemporary choruses is replaced by the beats per minute (BPM) of the 'dance scene'. At one end of the spectrum music can be the gentle ambient dance or simple chants and liturgical songs; at the other, the full-blooded Techno and

Acid or Rave. The music provides a backdrop to everything that happens: readings, video images and prayers all take place over it. This is an area of flourishing creativity; as many groups find that nothing available quite fits their situation or style, they choose to write and compose their own. The range of instruments used is also diverse and varied. A friend of mine joked, 'If you've seen it on *Later with Jules Holland* then it's in an alternative service somewhere.' There is more than an element of truth in this as groups experiment creatively with different sounds and ideas.

RITUALS

Another striking characteristic of culture-specific worship is the use of ritual. Often this can be in the form of simple personal acts: moulding clay, washing feet, lighting a candle, taking a stone, anointing with oil, tasting honey; or it can be more collective experiences of movement or dancing. Alongside this there is the larger liturgical ritual – the whole shape of the service through which the congregation is guided. Many things can stand at the core of the worship: ritual, extended sung praise, Holy Spirit ministry, maybe the sacraments of communion or baptism, or perhaps a time of teaching either incorporated into the ritual or as a more or less participatory presentation.

LAYERING

All the characteristics described in the previous paragraphs do not happen during the service in a linear fashion as they do in mainstream contemporary and traditional worship. Rather, they happen simultaneously. We often talk about a hymn sandwich: hymn–reading–hymn–sermon–hymn–prayers. Culture-specific worship is more akin to an American subway-style sandwich: there are half a dozen different things in there and you get some of each with every bite. The plan for morning service at the Lambeth Palace day on new/alternative worship has six column headings: Words, Video, Slides, Music, Action, People. These offer six layers of potential simultaneous activity within the service.

This characteristic multi-layering, where things happen simultaneously, is one of the features which separates alternative worship from youth congregations and youth churches.

PARTICIPATION AND BELONGING

Moving on from what happens within culture-specific worship to the structures existing behind the event, we find other differences from the mainstream.

> Everybody has the chance to take part in the service (music, reading, prayers etc.) which helps everyone to feel they as an individual have a positive part to play. The use of video, recorded music and drama in addition to the prayers, bible reading and liturgy of usual church services increase the ways in which young people can meet with God and each other and explore their faith.[8]

> The services are a good opportunity for young people to be involved in the planning and organizing of a meeting which is aimed at their needs and interests.[9]

> It was incredible, I loved the music, I experienced God, it was a dream come true and the people were real, normal, not the usual church types. They accepted and valued me for who I was.[10]

> There is a strong feeling of friendship and trust among the group and new members and their views are always welcomed and appreciated.[11]

> For me it was a place I could take an active role in worship leading and watch others do the same. Having more of a role than just drama or bible reading as it is in some churches.[12]

These two characteristics of active participation and a strong sense of belonging and being valued appear to go hand in hand. Participation is more than giving young people jobs to do; active participation challenges us to ask some difficult questions.

- To what extent do, or can, youth workers allow participation in youth work (the worship service) on terms determined by the young people they are seeking to serve?

- To what extent are the aims of the youth worker and the agency for whom she/he is working synonymous with the expectations of the young people?

- To what extent are youth workers prepared to relinquish power and control?

- To what extent are youth workers conscious of the inherent dependency which exists in their relationship with young people?[13]

As these questions are worked out in practice, there will be a real transfer of power and control. The sense of ownership of the service by the young people will grow, leading to the formulation of an agenda which addresses their issues and hence also to a worship service where the young people feel they belong not only because they attend and take part but because it is addressing their own spiritual agenda.

SUMMARY

Pulling these threads together, we find that culture-specific worship is highly visual, it involves a range of musical genres, it is strongly participatory, developing new forms of ritual as well as organization, and is characterized by a strong sense of community and purpose.

The value of culture-specific worship

Not everyone is so positive about what is happening in worship, as the Archbishop's Commission on Church Music noted. One of the people who wrote to it 'had little time for "religious observance indistinguishable from . . . forms of commercial entertainment"'; others wondered whether God's Glory could be adequately expressed 'by the tawdry words and music of modern pop culture' . . . 'traditional reverent worship turned into a jolly social discotheque atmosphere'.[14]

Or, as Lord Runcie commented recently,

> Some contemporary forms of worship are very bad at doing the one thing worship should do – lifting ourselves into a better world, into a more serious attitude to life . . . I regret people are not worshipping as they once did but turning worship into something fashionable – an ecclesiastical version of a health farm is a danger.[15]

The question of whether the tawdry words and music of popular culture can express God's glory could be seen as one of taste and preference, as in other areas of music. For example, only about 3 per cent of the population listen to Radio 3; a much higher percentage listen to Radios 1 and 2.

To argue that worship is only a matter of taste and preference is to concede too much ground, for it is also a matter of theology. It is our theology that will determine our view of creation and creativity. Did God make things good, or do we have a view of the world where only the spiritual internals are good and the externals are evil? If we believe that we are stewards of the creativity of God then that creativity can be seen somewhere in all culture and popular culture. Similarly, our theological understanding of incarnation will determine our response and mission approaches to groups of people. Do we stand aloof and say that if anyone would like to come and worship with us in the way that worship is being done, would they come? Or do we engage with the culture, with its grey areas and difficult questions? Jesus was constantly rebuked by the Pharisees for spending time with the tawdry publicans and prostitutes of local popular culture and not with the élite who could teach him a thing or two about God.

Far from failing to transform one's perspective, much culture-specific worship does draw us into the presence of God, lifting our spirit and transforming our attitude. It can 'Quicken the conscience by the holiness of God, to feed the mind with the truth of God, to purge the mind with the beauty of God, to open the heart to the love of God, to devote the will to the purpose of God.'[16]

Or in the words of Sarah, a student teacher,

> A friend persuaded me to go to my first Lifetime service. It was held in the crypt of Worcester Cathedral and its theme was Celtic Christianity. From the atmosphere that was created, the friendliness of these strangers (now my best friends) and being able to appreciate what was being said, it inspired me to rediscover my faith.

3

Getting behind the scenes

We have seen in the previous chapter that culture-specific worship is expressed in a variety of forms and styles and within a variety of contexts. As we have discovered, this is not a single phenomenon but rather appears to be the expression of a variety of different undercurrents and influences both within and upon the Church. In this chapter we shall try to identify these underlying influences. I have divided them into four categories:

- Ecclesiological
- Technological
- Theological
- Cultural

Ecclesiological influences

There have been a number of changes in the way we think about the Church and our practice of the Church, which have been formative in the development of culture-specific worship.

THE RISE IN NUMBER OF FULL-TIME CHURCH YOUTH WORKERS

The last decade has seen an exponential rise in the number of full-timers. It is estimated that there are over 500 in the Church of England alone. There are a variety of reasons for this growth.

- ***Declining numbers of clergy*** Churches that would once have had one or more assistant clergy no longer do so. The workload has not reduced, so lay specialists are employed as administrators, youth ministers and children's workers in order to free the minister for what the congregation sees as his or her primary responsibility.

● **Parental concerns** The world beyond the Church is a dangerous place full of sex, drugs and demons. Church young people drop out at an alarming rate, so safety is strong motivation for investment in Christian youth ministry. The Church is there to provide a safe alternative to the world outside.

● **Finance available** The last ten years have seen many wealthy churches' income rise faster than quota and inflation, therefore the finances have been made available to employ additional staff.

● **Keeping up with St Jones's** Many churches would of course deny that their reason for needing a full-time youth worker is that the church up the road or next door has one. However, when they see the work that such people are able to do, and the impact they make, there is often a strong desire to replicate this ministry in their own parish.

● **Mission imperative** We are in the Decade of Evangelism and young people are one of the groups under-represented in our churches. There is a strong desire and commitment to evangelize young people but an equal lack of confidence, knowledge and experience of how to do it. Employing a youth specialist can provide the missing requirements.

● **Lack of leaders** Due to time pressure, lack of people in the right age bracket and of the right ability, it is harder for churches to find people to be volunteer church youth leaders.

This rise in the number of full-time leaders has been the provider of people power and energy for the formation of many culture-specific worship services. This is not to imply that these are not possible where there is not the input of a full-timer. The Nine O'clock Service released people through community living; others have done the same through a much more shared ministry approach. However, as many full-time youth workers are in their 20s and 30s, they are often more aware of the culture gap between the Church and people of their own age and younger. When they experience the Church close up, they often find it at best highly frustrating and at worst disillusioning. All these factors underline the need to find new ways of missioning youth cultures.

The impact of full-time youth workers is felt both internally within the Church's life and also externally in relation to other Churches and youth groups.

Internally If a church invests a considerable amount of money in a worker, they are obviously going to be more inclined to take seriously what that worker says. Full-timers are in the advantageous position of being able to educate PCCs, elderships, house groups, prayer meetings etc. about the needs of young people and the issues facing them. They are also able to educate and influence their ministers and thereby, often unwittingly, change the balance of power within the church. This realignment of power combined with education makes structural changes and new initiatives within worship more possible and opens the door for new forms, styles and times of services.

Externally The arrival of full-time youth workers on the scene has made it possible for individual congregations to put on the type of event which once could only have been staged by a Youth For Christ centre, deanery youth committee or similar, as they would have been the ones with the resources. Events such as concerts, rallies, schools missions and youth celebrations are now put on by individual churches or even youth groups.

This movement down to individual churches for the organization and holding of events has had the added impact of bringing the local church face to face with the problem of following up those who are converted at these initiatives and, more specifically, the integration or non-integration of these young people into their worship structures. This creates the opportunity for new things to happen or not to happen. When the young people who come to the monthly event begin to see it as their church, rather than moving towards integration into the main meeting of the congregation, it is often difficult for the congregation to react and respond and almost impossible for many to accept that the solution might mean planting a youth congregation, church or service.

In addition to the impact that full-timers have had internally and externally on the structures of the local churches, they have, of course, a major impact on the young people. Here is someone on their side. He or she is often only half a generation older and has similar attitudes. This gives a massive boost of confidence to young people. They have an opportunity to participate in a huge range of new experiences, projects, training courses etc. They have an advocate.

This is not to say that churches without full-time youth workers cannot or do not provide these things. Many churches do great youth work with tribes of committed volunteers. Either way, the result is young people who are more experienced, better trained, better prepared for Christian service and leadership and who feel able to take on the responsibilities of leading or taking an active part in a youth congregation. Churches and congregations who train up and prepare their young people from an early age are better equipped to church plant further along the line.

DECLINE

The National Church Census, the surveys and studies by Lesley Francis, and Peter Brierley's *Reaching and Keeping Teenagers*[1] have shown the dramatic decline in the numbers of young people and young adults worshipping in the Church in this country. These figures are so unambiguous that even taking into account other factors such as the total drop in the number of teenagers in society, there has been and continues to be a massive decline in young people and young adults belonging to the Church. There has also been a decline in the number of older young people involved in youth organizations in general. We need to be aware of this move away from structured organizations, as well as actively responding to it.

The decline obviously has a number of effects. First, parents are increasingly anxious for their children's spiritual futures. Most Christian parents hope that their children will grow up to be practising Christians. A growing number have realized that in the majority of cases this just does not happen. They want to find programmes that will deliver what they seek. They can see what attracts young people to other churches or individual services and, even if they may have reservations about theology, they will want to see something similar replicated or included as part of the youth programme offered by their own church.

Second, church leaders are increasingly willing to try new things. Leaders have seen young people leaving the church in their teens and twenties in ever-increasing numbers over the last three decades. So far, there has not been any evident return from this group in later life. The statistics have blown out of the water the theory that it does not matter if worshippers drift away in their teens because they will come back when they get older. Church leaders are increasingly, if still unwillingly, having to come to terms with the fact that if these people are lost from the Church in their teens and twenties then they are probably lost for good. Church leaders are also aware that the problems and reasons for this huge departure from the Church go much deeper than the style of the music or the topic of the sermon, and they are therefore willing to allow opportunities for experiment.

Participation

Youth work increasingly emphasises participation. Peer ministry has become the equivalent of secular youth work's peer training. Young people are used in youth work projects like Christmas Cracker and Wash for Dosh to taking responsibility for a huge variety of tasks: accounting, marketing, press relations, speaking to local churches, leading Bible studies and worship. Through Family Services they will also, as children, have read lessons, led intercessions, or been involved in dance, drama or presentations. Despite this wealth of experience, which not all our adult congregational members share, they are relatively underused as they get older. In the wider church their gifts are unused and often undervalued, possibly for fear of exploitation or through ignorance. We have a huge resource of young people and young adults who are unable to use their gifts in much of the worship in our churches.

A generation ago, many in a similar position moved out of the mainstream denominations to form the New Churches.

> The house church movement consists of people who 20 years ago were in the mainstream denominations who were unhappy. It's another group who have reconstructed church. They were marginalised and disempowered . . . the older generation in the mainstream denominations had a stranglehold on power, so these people went elsewhere.[2]

Going elsewhere does not always solve the problem. It can simply recreate it somewhere else, with a new generation marginalizing and disempowering the next. This is not such a problem for those churches which emphasise church-planting and use the new generation to provide leadership in the new congregations.

Elsewhere, some people question the whole structure and nature of our expressions of the Church:

> In the worship of 'alternative' services, for technological as much as cultural reasons, the role and necessity of liturgical leadership is being called into question . . . Beyond the practical questioning of the role of liturgical president, there lies the deeper cultural questioning of the associated views of the church and its ministry which have been supported and ritually affirmed by this liturgical role. Many of the service groups are small enough to act by consensus, even if this is never pain free. Others are experimenting with some kind of structured-in democracy.[3]

In practical terms, this has meant groups experimenting with new structures and a quest for authentic forms of leadership for today's culture.

DISAFFECTION

> Last week, I was with a group of teenagers. One of them had been watching a TV programme about AIDS in Uganda. 'I think it is disgusting,' she said, 'it's disgusting

that when people are dying in Africa and all those children being orphaned – and all that has been happened in Bosnia too – it's disgusting that all the Church does is argue about who should be clergy.[4]

A generation has grown up with a vision of a Church at odds with their experience. Steve Chalke comments:

The rising generation . . . unable to reconcile their developing spiritual and world views with the expression of church that they find themselves part of, will declare their independence, this time not over issues of worship, style, language and clothing, but over those of ecology, justice, world concern and lifestyle and will leave to form a new expression of church.[5]

This disaffection is not just confined to the rising generation. Many in their 20s and 30s have discovered that suggestions from young adults' forums, youth councils, youth covenants and declarations, youth members on the PCC and other such well-meaning initiatives have for the greater part made no difference to the structures and power relationships within churches. I was at diocesan synod only a few weeks ago and there was no one there aged under 30 and 80 per cent were aged over 50.

Abuse of these power relationships by church leaders is widespread. Here abuse means the misuse of power and consequent maltreatment of young people and young adults. I am not talking about sexual abuse, although sadly it is all too common, but rather the systematic undermining of individuals and their vision of the Church. 'Spiritual abuse happens when a person is given a poor self-image, a poor image of God, or is controlled or manipulated by the Church.'[6]

There are too many hurt people for this to be just a case of problematic individual leaders. Rather, it is a consequence of poor structures occupied by too many insecure, tired, defensive leaders who have undue expectations placed upon them. It is often said that you cannot be disillusioned if you do not have any illusions in the first place. That is OK for the cynics, but there is a different vision. A vision of a Church that is open, inclusive, socially active; where there is community and shared leadership; where people are built up, empowered and encouraged to spiritually grow; where there is the freedom to fail, freedom to question and disagree; and, most of all, where there is such evident love that people ask how they can experience what these Christians have got.

The reason the NOS was so successful was not only its ability to engage the culture, but also the high vision of the Church it offered to people – a vision that is well worth making our goal.

THE FAILURE OF FAMILY WORSHIP (FOR YOUNG PEOPLE)

Family Worship and all-age services can be traced back to the 1920s and 30s but really took off in the 1960s when a number of Churches began experimenting with new informal liturgies and types of worship. These liturgies expanded and have become institutionalized and much time and energy has gone into developing all-age resources. But it is not all that simple, as Penny Frank describes so bluntly:

> I think at gut level that all age something or other ought to happen regularly within the life of the church . . . It would be true to say I feel really disheartened about the all age scene at the moment . . . It seems that people don't comment back on any other services the way they feel free to comment back on the all age scene and it is a completely harsh assessment.[7]

This negativity is a common experience for many who arrange or lead all-age services. I can remember seeing feedback sheets for an all-age congregation and was surprised by the power and negativity of many of the comments – and not only from those attending the service. It seems that although visitors often enjoy and get a lot out of all-age services, even when they are done well there is an apparent failure to deliver for the wider congregation.

Sadly, this is also often true for all-age services and young people. This is not always to do with the worship itself but with the young person's perception of it. If a young person attended all-age services as a child and participated actively, enjoying and engaging with the worship etc., then they may be less keen when they are changing from child to adult. This will be part of a more general rejection of childish things. If all-age worship is perceived by them to be childish, it too will be rejected. Even if there is no rejection in this instance, it is unlikely that young people will drag along their non-Christian friends to something they feel self-conscious about because it is childish. To be successfully 'all-age', the service must contain childlike or child-oriented elements and this can sometimes pose problems for our teenagers.

For older young people, young adults and single people, the nuclear family base of much all-age worship can equally be a problem. All-age worship has failed to deliver what it promises. This failure again acts as an influence on culture-specific worship; worship must be inclusive, not leaving people out who do not fit neatly into the nuclear family emphasis. Similarly, it must not be childish or cringingly embarrassing if it wants to engage with those who do not want to be butterflies or participate in quizzes.

SEEKER-SENSITIVE SERVICES

The dramatic success of Willow Creek Community Church in holding seeker-friendly services for those beyond the fringe of the Church and drawing people into faith and the life of the Church has become well known. Although often geared to the middle-aged and expressed with the slickness of presentation expected by the baby-boomer generation, these cringe-free outreach services are a form of culture-specific worship although they are not targeted at young people.

Seeker-sensitive services have a carefully crafted mixture of material presented up-front, talks which focus on connecting everyday life issues with the Christian faith, and good quality drama, dance etc. Sometimes there is video input and songs sung to the audience/congregation, with perhaps one or two for them to join in. The whole emphasis is on engaging with people where they are and this is reflected heavily in terms of the issues addressed and the style of presentation.

The five features of Willow Creek are:

● Anonymity for those attending;

● Creativity rather than blandness or banality;

● Suitability – the material is relevant to the target group;

● Excellence to reduce the 'cringe factor';

● Integrity – word and action match up.

I would question whether anonymity should be a characteristic of Christian worship, but the other four features are an excellent self-assessment test that we could run on any service. Is it creative? Suitable? Excellent? Has it integrity? The growth of seeker-friendly services also benefits other culture-specific services by educating people to other possibilities, challenging many assumptions and so creating an environment in which more creative things can be done.

Technological influences

The last ten years have seen an explosion in the use of technology in a variety of ways. The range of hardware and software now available is enormous. The world of computer-generated graphics, video filming, mixing and editing, sound amplification, sequencing, reproduction and recording, video and digital projection, can all be done 'at home' in ways that could not have been imagined twenty years ago. The cost of equipment has also massively reduced. What could not have been imagined twenty years ago could not have been afforded ten years ago. Today, a home PC can do what used to require a studio, and the starting price of a video projector is only £1,000 today as against £7,000 a decade or so ago (although prices are rising again as the quality and brightness of even the most basic models are increased). The videofilm recorder has not only shrunk in size to a camcorder but also in price: 'The moving multimedia mode of communication has become two way. Long disenfranchized groups now have access to the dominant means of communication and expression through multimedia. The church is one such group among many.'⁸

The speed at which this type of change takes place is still gathering pace. Technology does not stop; no sooner is one thing produced than it is seemingly instantaneously superseded and outdated. One effect of this is a sense of insecurity and loss for some, but for others it creates opportunities for creativity and expression. They are now able to participate actively in worship whereas before they were only spectators.

The use of technology opens doors to worship contributions previously unavailable. Culture-specific worship using technological advances such as projected video clips and loops, computer graphics, DAT (digital) recordings, slide images etc., will involve a wide range of people in planning, preparing and producing the whole experience. People are able to contribute even before they feel able to participate actively to the worship itself.

This whole process has the interesting effect of changing views of worship. All of a sudden it has the added dimension of being something in which we can participate directly as co-workers rather than mere spectators. Participation produces feelings of belonging and ownership and this is one of the important and attractive characteristics of culture-specific worship.

The other technological innovation that impacts on the scene is the Internet. Much of the discussion and debate about alternative worship takes place through web sites and e-mail. The alternative worship magazine *Re Generate* was short-lived in paper form but the debate moved on to the Net. Some of the useful web sites and e-mail addresses for organizations are included in Appendix.

Theological influences

There have been a number of influential theologies, movements and spiritualities which have impacted on the Church and influenced culture-specific worship. The first group of these are often referred to as contextual theologies, and provide models for the inculturation of Christianity into post-modern society.

LIBERATION THEOLOGY

Liberation Theology has its origins in Latin America. It

> attempts to reflect on the experience and meaning of the
> faith based on the commitment to abolish injustice and to
> build a new society; this theology must be verified by the
> practice of that commitment, by active, effective partici-
> pation in the struggle which the exploited social classes
> have taken against the oppressors . . . to subvert an order
> of injustice – with the fullness with which Christ loved
> us.[9]

Liberation Theology has brought us the concept of Base Christian
Communities: small groups of Christians meeting together to look
at Scripture in their own context, to worship, celebrate and act
for the good of the community. These groups have also popular-
ized the 'Experience, Reflection, Action, Reflection' method of
studying theology (also known as the Pastoral Cycle).[10] This
method has four repeated stages:

● It might begin, in any of our situations, with the sharing of
an experience, situation or action. For example, a group of
young people new to the Christian faith, who find church
boring or irrelevant, might share a feeling of not fitting in or
not feeling wanted at church. This is their experience.

● The next stage would be a reflective one: not just a friendly
chat, sharing of information, or an 'Oprah Winfrey' type of
open discussion, but a journey through our part in the situation. How we feel, how others feel. The process involves
investigation, prayer, worship, Scripture, searching and asking questions. If we stop the process at this point, unsolved
but 'better for the airing' and 'thanks for listening', or end
with 'the Bible says lump it', then our young people do not
grow or learn to do theology. This process of doing their theology will become part of their tools for faith, part of what
keeps them questioning, applying their faith and growing
with each challenge that confronts them. Without this kind
of faith and personal development they will be unlikely to

stay at church unless they are psychologically in need of a 'parent'.

● The third stage is one of related action. This is the doing part of theology. We are not simply hearers of the word, but doers (cf. James 1.22). The action we could take might consist of a series of experimental responses in the light of our reflection. It might involve the group holding a joint event with adults from the church; experimenting with their own worship; explaining the difficulties they are facing with church leaders; or some other response. All the possible responses will be researched and evaluated as part of the reflective process and it may well be that these will be discarded and the decision made to 'stick it out'.

● The last stage is another one of reflection on the action taken – or not taken. The group has been brought round full circle and now has another situation and bundle of feelings and responses to reflect upon.

This method of working has the added benefit of gently enabling people to move away from client–provider styles of ministry, away from dependency and the inherent risks of abuse.

As with any grass-roots, bottom-up movement, the ideas of Liberation Theology cannot be totally translated into a different culture, but the process of a more active style of theology is detectable within the alternative worship scene. As Pete Ward describes:

> The young people meet in friendship groups which reflect the culture of their particular area. This allows them to talk about being Christians in terms which make sense in their own local environment and culture. We encourage them to help each other and support each other in prayer, but we also give them time to reflect as a group on passages of the bible.[11]

The influence of a Liberation Theology style of thought in culture-specific worship is a subtle one. It provides a framework which can free up methods of discipleship and spiritual growth and can also handle the democratization of worship.

FEMINIST THEOLOGY

> Women have together discovered and expressed how
> their experience of being subordinated tallies with so
> much of the yearning of God for self expression. This has
> meant that we can now see how much of our theology
> has been constructed from male experience.[12]

The development of Feminist Theology reflects the development
of feminism in arts, the media and psychoanalysis in the 1970s
and 1980s. Its influence on culture-specific worship is through
both its challenge to masculine hegemony within the theology of
the Church and the impact which feminism has on post-modern
art and popular culture.

We can see how the feminist influence has also begun to
determine some of the practices within the culture-specific
congregation. It has influence because of the 'physicality of
Christian feminist activities – dancing, breathing, touching'[13].
The incorporation of these physical elements into the rites in
culture-specific worship helps to give it an embodiment that is
often lacking in traditional liturgy. It has a closeness, an intimacy
and an approachability that challenges.

'Many women who come to Feminist Spirituality Groups, come
exhausted. They want to affirm the reality of the spiritual, they
often want desperately to cling on to a faith which enriches them
and they find the going tough.'[14] This state of affairs reaches
beyond those in touch with feminist spirituality to the many that
are hurting. Taking this on board is one of the characteristics
which makes alternative worship attractive both within and
beyond the Church.

ENVIRONMENTAL THEOLOGY

This is often called creation spirituality and is linked to Matthew
Fox, who draws on a range of medieval mystics, some Christian
as well as tribal Shaman, to help rediscover ritual and mysticism
in the Western world. He also emphasizes what he calls the 'original blessing' in contrast to original sin, Jesus as a son of God

helping people to find the God-force or Cosmic Christ and through this connect with the god within to stop the environmental apocalypse and develop a sense of awe for the planet and creation. Depending on your own standpoint, Environmental Theology either tries to offer 'a holistic Christian theology which addresses the destruction of the planet, patriarchy and sexism in the church and the need for a new mysticism and a reinvigorated ritual to communicate in post-modern society';[15] or it is New Age and either harmless or highly dodgy, depending on your theology; or it is neo-paganism in disguise and to be avoided at all costs.

One of the problems with creation spirituality is that we can all too easily approach it from these entrenched standpoints and so either miss out on useful insights or swallow whole some unhealthy ones.

Taking another look at Environmental Theology devoid of Matthew Fox, it does ask us questions about how we experience God's revelation in creation. How can we use the sense of awe it inspires? We experience a beautiful sunset, a mountain walk, a rainswept coast, and we have to respond. Many culture-specific worship services and events use visual images drawing on this creative revelation, while others seek more tactile and sense-based experiences of worship that touch on and draw out the creative within us, recognizing that God has made us part of creation as well as its stewards. Environmental concerns are more than just an 'issue' to many. The way we use and abuse the earth is for them a cause for great concern, as Be Real insists: 'Of course sin and redemption were important, but not all consuming – the fact that the world was facing an environmental crisis was just as important and appeared to be being ignored.'[16]

The second group of theologies which influence culture-specific worship are a more diverse variety of movements which remain, however, within the mainstream of church life.

CELTIC SPIRITUALITY

Celtic Christianity has some similarities with Environmental Theology: it has a holistic approach to spirituality and faith but sits firmly within orthodox Christianity and is highly influential not just on the culture-specific worship scene but also within the mainstream of Christian worship. The Celtic tradition emphasizes God's glory in all creation and Jesus as head of all. As the *Iona Community Worship Book* puts it in its introduction:

> Our whole life, we believe, is a search for wholeness. We desire to be fully human, with no division into the sacred and secular. We desire to be fully present to God who is fully present to us, whether in our neighbour or in the political and social activity of the world around us, whether in the fields of culture or of economics, and whether in prayer and praise together or in the very centre and soul of our being.[17]

The influence of Celtic spirituality is not only on the liturgy, ritual and song which originate within and have been adapted or adopted by culture-specific congregations, but also on ways of thinking and doing. There is a desire for a 'whole life' expression of faith, for a Christianity that is not left in the porch on the way out of church but is more connected to God's world and draws on traditions and history, not just experience.

THE CHARISMATIC MOVEMENT

Now firmly established within the mainstream of the Church in this country, the various strands within the charismatic movement are both embraced and rejected by those within the culture-specific worship scene.

For some, the space created by moving out from the mainstream is one in which they are free to explore the use of the gifts of the Spirit, seek God in intimate worship, experience healing and deliverance, use prophetic gifts etc. They regard the gifts of the Spirit as manifestations of the kingdom that help us demonstrate the reality of the power and presence of God to those beyond the

Church. Many of the Church plants and youth congregations use mainstream charismatic music, and some of the music developed in culture-specific worship has been incorporated back into the mainstream.

For others the charismatic movement produces a range of different responses. Some are unhappy with 'the charismatic approach of a selfish, personal relationship with God'[18] that accompanies those who judge things by what they get out of them. It is all too common to hear people coming away from a major charismatic event defining it in these terms; either, 'I didn't get anything out of it' or 'I was really blessed (by what I got out of it)', although one could see this response as more a product of a post-modern culture than of the charismatic worship itself.

Others find that the concepts and theologies expressed in the songs are not easily grasped or always helpful for those coming from outside the Church, and that the operation of charismatic gifts is sometimes a barrier.

Some are just disillusioned with the charismatic movement: they have been there, done that and are looking for an authentic expression of where they are in their journey of faith. There is a fairly steady stream of people falling out of charismatic evangelical churches feeling hurt, confused and abused and looking for new ways to worship and new communities to do so in.

There is also a question mark over whether some elements of charismatic worship perpetuate a child–parent relationship within the Church. Song lyrics such as 'I want you to hold me like my daddy never did . . . hold me, hold me father, never let me go, hold me tight, hold me close . . . hand in hand we'll run and play'[19] may be to some a reflection of an intimate relationship with a heavenly father, but from others it evokes a response of 'Isn't it time you grew up?'[20] As we move on in our faith, we move on from where we are; this is all part and parcel of faith development and where it leads us, but we shall come to this in more detail later on.

These concerns apart, it is clear that the charismatic movement has a number of important dimensions which have been drawn upon by some culture-specific congregations:

● Kingdom teaching, especially through the influence of John Wimber and the Vineyard, which recognizes that Jesus' message that the kingdom of God is at hand and breaking in is as relevant today as it was then. This breaking-in of the kingdom is demonstrated by 'signs and wonders' but also by a concern for justice and social issues.

● Spiritual gifting, which is more than every-member ministry: it is a realization that God gifts people in different and special ways, including the more familiar charismata. These gifts are not for personal glory or status but for building up the Church and for ministering beyond it into the community to demonstrate the presence of the kingdom.

● Worship resources. The charismatic movement produces a vast wealth of worship material, not just hymns and songs but also writings, videos, teaching, experiences and events.

In the next chapter we shall look more closely at the relationship between faith development, worship and culture. However, before we leave the charismatic movement we have to acknowledge the very powerful influence it has had on culture-specific worship, acting sometimes as a defining line between those who take on board what it stands for and those who reject its theology and teaching.

The Church-planting movement

This movement has grown increasingly in influence over the last two decades, since the first National Day Conference on Church-planting in May 1987, which demonstrated the importance of Church-planting in evangelism and Church growth strategies.

Church-planting is not just on the Anglican agenda and on the agendas of the other established denominations; it is also very much a part of New Church life. There are a number of strategies and initiatives to encourage Church growth through planting;

these include the Dawn 2000 strategy and Anglican Church-planting Initiatives. This enthusiasm for Church-planting has gone hand in hand with new ways of describing and understanding what is happening on the worship scene. There has been a lot of work on a life-cycle approach to Church reproduction investigations into the different types of Church-planting: is it to be a duplicate service? Is it to be congregation multiplication or a matter of building sharing? Is it a launch out into a satellite meeting, daughter church or adult church? What is the purpose of the plant? Is it a geographically unchurched area or an unreached people group? Is it a plant that will offer a specific worship style?

There has been much excellent work in this area undertaken by groups such as Youth With A Mission, the New Zealand Baptist Union etc., of value not just to culture-specific congregations but to the Church at large.

One of the concepts which Church-planting has brought us is the 'Homogeneous Unit Principle'. The homogenous unit is a section of society where all the members have some characteristic in common. It could be geography, language, ethnicity, history, culture, age or class. It makes people feel at home with one another and aware of their identity as a distinctive group. The homogeneous unit principle says that people most easily become Christians when they do not have to cross barriers of race, language or class. Homogeneous unit churches are the most effective in evangelism. However, this creates a problem: when we look at Scripture and read that there is neither Greek nor Jew, male nor female, slave nor free in Christ Jesus, how do we then reconcile trying to reach people within cultural boundaries?

The answer is all bound up with where we find the wholeness of the Church, which we shall look at in the next chapter; but it also comes from recognizing the need to move on and then out from ethnocentricity as part of our response to the gospel. The implications of this are far-reaching for culture-specific congregations because it provides the challenge to build relationships with the rest of the body of Christ, locally, cross-culturally and nationally. This, at the end of the day, is the way that most churches cope with the fact that they are culture-specific.

This affirmation of cultural specificity positively encourages cultural diversity, enhancing the creativity of worship and encouraging authenticity and freedom not to settle for the lowest common denominator of drab mediocrity into which worship all too easily descends.

Cultural influences

What are the influences in the wider culture which affect and influence what is happening in culture-specific worship? In this section I shall not be looking at the variations in sub-culture concerned with the 'meaning of style' but at the broader cultural changes which shape the world we operate in and which we often fail to take on board when we make decisions as the Church. This is partly because we have constructed our own sub-culture and partly because of a tendency for the Church to invest energy in keeping things as they are.

As culture-specific congregations are by definition much more responsive to these cultural changes, it will be useful to identify some of them and look at their potential influences on what is happening.

Post-modernism

The last twenty years have seen a major change in culture. The pervasive cultural view since the Enlightenment (modernism) is being washed away as certainly as a sandcastle before an incoming tide. Gone are reason, science and progress, with man as the author of his own destiny, able to solve any problem. Gone is the bigger picture, the absolute explanation. Post-modernism is replacing this with a more holistic approach based on intuition: image (the screen) supersedes text (the book), subjectivity supersedes objectivity, networks and grass-roots movements displace organizations and the externals of style replace the internals of depth.

> Post modernism has flowed right out of the musky corridors of academia into the world of popular culture; it is on the pages of youth magazines, on CD boxes and the

fashion pages of *Vogue*. It has abolished the old distinction between 'high' and 'low' art, and created new art forms out of things like music videos, urban graffiti and computer graphics. Few things could, in fact, better sum up the postmodern situation better than the term 'virtual reality', for it is a world in which the old certainties are dissolving.[21]

The implications of this for the Church are massive, because today's Church, in both its liberal and evangelical forms, has grown up with modernism. Both wings have their origins in the post-Enlightenment period, one as a reaction against the other; they are opposite sides of the same coin, having different but equally rational views of society and faith. Much of culture-specific worship is about enculturing the gospel, with post-modern communities and groups finding ways to express faith through the use of new rituals, visual images and journeying. This post-modern expression of the Church allows individuals the space to do this for themselves, making their own connections and interpretations to construct a more personal and holistic faith. For those who are used to the more didactic methods of spiritual growth, this may sound rather too much of a 'pick and mix' spirituality; I can hear that 'Church Parent' voice saying 'Is it sound, Patrick?' To many this is not an issue; they have already rejected the 'Church Parent' and are seeking authentic spirituality. Furthermore, image and intuition can be just as valid for drawing us into the presence of God as logical reason.

CULTURE ABUSE

This term has been coined by Richard Eckersley, an Australian Federal Government policy consultant and researcher, to describe the issues affecting young people: crime, drugs, and the rise of eating disorders, suicide, unemployment and mental disorders. 'Our culture', he says, 'arguably fails to meet the most fundamental requirements of any culture; to provide a sense of belonging and purpose and so a sense of meaning and self worth, and a moral framework to guide our conduct.'[22]

Cultural abuse is not restricted to Australia; *Youth A Part* identified a further range of issues important to young people: bullying, work and training, not having a job, homes and housing, drink and drugs, being a victim, family tensions, sexuality. How about the Church? Do we do any better than society at large or are we part of the problem for our young people? And as for culture-specific congregations . . . it's all very well being part of a nice bunch of white middle-class graduates in their 20s and 30s, but is that really the Church for those who are hurting? Just a thought.

As a youth worker I see a huge gap between the world of many young people and the world of the person in the pew. Sometimes it is just impossible to envisage the two making much of a connection. There is no way that the Church can begin to feel what it is like to be a young person today, even if it really wants to or sees the need for it.

The despair of this situation challenges us; there must be other ways of being and doing the Church which take into account our differences and our cultures. Jesus calls us to build his Church. How we have done this has often had more to do with us than with him. Culture-specific worship has the potential to address some of the problems and create spaces where there can be a sense of belonging, purpose, meaning and self-worth.

DANCE MUSIC

As soon as house music kicked in in the middle of the 1980s and the club scene took shape, the Church's relationship with the music of popular culture changed.

> Rock and Christianity never mixed too well . . . for a start there was discomfort at using the devil's music to get people closer to God . . . Rock music is all about rebellion, against society, against whatever, but in the case of Christian rock this doesn't work. The medium and message are at odds. Christianity says be nice, rock says f*** school, let's get pissed. In other words Christian rock just sounds stupid. Rave, house, club culture is a whole different kettle of fish. It's a participatory activity, it's a

collective experience. One where you feel empathy with those around you and is based on a sense of disorientation and losing yourself. These are also essential elements of a successful act of worship . . . If a Christian DJ is playing or a non believer, could you tell? House music is a perfect vehicle for speech samples and visuals of a religous nature. And it won't look stupid.[23]

Not only is house/rave/club music the dominant music style in youth culture, it is also a medium that Christians can participate in at the forefront, rather than with a poor reflection of the real thing as has been the case with rock.

MILLENNIALISM

There is an almost eschatological sense to much of what is happening in society as we build up towards the end of the millennium; no doubt there will be a post-millennial hangover to follow. Thoughts and predictions welcome here! This is evident not just from the rise of cults and sects, but in society at large.

Predictions are a dangerous business, as all those who have prophesied renewal in the United Kingdom over the last twenty years can testify. However, we can see a growing interest in fictional apocalyptic writings and this will probably increase vastly as we approach the millennium. Specific predictions of the end times are often associated with cults and sects, and culture-specific congregations need to be wary of being dragged into or associated with this type of thing.

There is another side to this: the second millennium commemorates Christ's birth. There are many initiatives, projects and programmes planned to coincide with this. It is a time of increasing interest in both the Christian faith and Jesus' life and its actual meaning. Culture-specific worship is creating the environment of faith to respond to this growing need. Not only should we aim 'to have a Youth Church in every city'[24] but we need new expressions of the Church in every town and local village.

All these different influences are like invisible forces, creating and acting upon the culture-specific congregation. How different communities and individuals respond to these influences depends on their own circumstance and experiences.

SEARCHINGS

As well as these external forces, I believe that there are some internal ones acting within young people and adults. For want of a better name I will call these 'searchings' – those desires of the inner self for which we seek fulfilment in the spiritual life. Where a church fails to meet these there is a lostness and a distance between where it is and where people want it to be. When this distance becomes too great, people find it no longer possible to remain in any meaningful way within that church. The following is by no means an exclusive list, but this searching includes:

- The search for community: where we can share and care for one another even when that means pain and sacrifice.

- The search for acceptance: where I can be me and still be welcomed and included.

- The search for authenticity: where no one has to or is pretending, where there is a realness to the spiritual that is more than skin deep.

- The search for sacred space: a place that is holy, where the reality of God can be experienced, through the senses and with the silence.

- The search for spiritual growth: where the growth within me is part of a deepening relationship with God.

These searchings are what have drawn women and men down the years to Christ, because in him they see their fulfilment. Their frequent absence from contemporary church life is a sign of how far we have drifted off-course. Culture-specific worship is in this sense only drawing us back to where we should be.

Pulling the threads together, we can see that any individual culture-specific congregation or service will be an expression of the various ways that these and other influences have acted upon and within it. The wide range of factors and the differing ways groups respond to them (some for example would embrace Environmental Theology, others reject it, and vice versa for the charismatic gifts) helps explain why we have such divergence of activity within culture-specific worship.

4

What is worship?
What is the Church?

'Now let us worship God,' announces the worship group leader at the beginning of a twenty-minute block of songs. Does this mean that the opening prayer, reading, confession and other proceedings were not worship or that the sermon or prayers or whatever will follow will not be? What about the midweek gatherings for prayer or Mass; are they worship? Is it worship when we live out our faith in the everyday happenings of life?

What is worship?

One of the problems that we face when we talk about worship is that so much of the 'worship debate' in the 1970s and 80s was centred around music and the gradual transformation of hymns and liturgical words into choruses and music group formats. Following this, we now find it difficult to define worship in the broader sense which is so much more than purely liturgy or singing. We may acknowledge that worship means 'to kiss the hand of Jesus', in the words of the songwriter Ishmael,[1] but often we limit our definition to the songs that will be in the service.

Alternatively we might talk about intimacy or being in God's presence, but again this is often related to that part of the service where a series of songs sung back-to-back create a mood which is seen to be conducive to such worship. This is not to say that the experience of God's presence is just the result of a mood created by the music; I simply use this illustration to highlight the narrowing and subjectivizing which I feel has taken place within the realm of worship. 'When we talk about worship in some circles we get stuck on singing and music and that expression is it.'[2]

Often these worship debates can feel like two people sitting in a room deciding on the colour of its walls and not realizing that there is also the whole house and the garden to explore. Let us try to get out of the house and explore.

God is. The starting point of worship has to be a realization of who God is; and as we get an inkling of the enormity of who God is, our response is awe. God cannot be labelled, boxed, controlled, cajoled, trivialized or owned. God is. 'I am who I am.'[3] As we continue to focus on God our perspective begins to change. My significance, desires, preferences become inconsequential as I try to respond to the God who is. This active response, this worship, is spoken of in Scripture as an active, doing thing. It involves prostrating, paying devotion, venerating, serving, being pious, sacrificing . . . but it is also more than awe and we need to hold other dynamics in balance. 'You who were once far off have been brought near in the blood of Christ.'[4] The God who is, is Jesus, who has redeemed us, giving us cause to celebrate. Furthermore, the God who is, is also the Holy Spirit and that Holy Spirit is in me changing me into the likeness of Jesus.

Let us begin by taking a brief look at how worship has developed in the last 30 years. The dominant form of worship 30 years ago was what I have called traditional; it still exists, not restricted to Anglicanism and Roman Catholicism but continuing in all the traditional denominations. Today, however, the dominant form is contemporary worship. This covers a range of more informal worship patterns, used by many of the mainline denominations and most of the New Churches. The third form of worship I call prospective: the patterns of worship that will be the mainstream worship of tomorrow, the prototypes of which are in use today.

TRADITIONAL

Traditional worship is characterized by beauty in building, music, liturgy, drawing on the historical resources of choral music and hymnody accompanied by organ and choir. Unhappy with the wholesale buying into contemporary culture, this view can be found on the editorial pages of some newspapers: 'By seeking to ape the world, and its transient trends and fashions, the church throws away the most powerful card it holds, its singularity.'[5] Traditional worship does not necessarily imply traditional theology or morality. There is no assumption of orthodoxy. Surprisingly, many of those who are most dogmatic about changes to historical forms and patterns of worship are most cavalier in their desire to jettison traditional morality and beliefs.

CONTEMPORARY

The contemporary church is of the 'carpet and chairs' variety. The pews are replaced by chairs, wooden floors by carpets, 'who at home does not have carpets' would be the argument of the contemporary. The songs are led by a worship group, the words are displayed by OHP, there are dancers, drama and coloured banners. 'In the contemporary church, the church organ was replaced by a band, liturgy was replaced with media and icons were removed to give a worship centre the look of a theatre.'[6]

Contemporary worship is in some ways the reverse of traditional worship; although modern in practice, it is often traditional in doctrine, supporting orthodox morality and doctrinal belief. It is those within the contemporary church movement who have been most concerned with church reorganization. This has been necessary in order to create space for the contemporary church practices of dance, drama, space for worship bands, sound equipment etc. The desire to worship in more comfortable surroundings is something they are quite happy to finance, even if it means sacrificial giving.

PROSPECTIVE

If contemporary worship is worship geared to the values enshrined by the 'baby-boom generation', then prospective worship is worship that reflects the values of Generation X – those following the baby-boom generation.

> Generation Xers want worship to be passionate and honest. They are more attracted to a coffee house concept of

worship than a theatre approach. Generation Xers view the boomers buy in to trendy approaches as superficial . . . having grown up in a post modern world generation Xers are seeking a more mystical religious experience as opposed to a rational didactic religion. Icons and symbols become an attraction for the Xer.[7]

Those seeking these new ways of worshipping find commercial Christian music second rate and passionless. The desire is for authenticity and participation as against entertainment and banality, alongside structures that enable and involve producing community and lasting relationships. The roots of this prospective worship may well lie in the alternative worship of today, but it could be that there are other paradigms, either within culture-specific worship or indeed running counter to culture-specificity, which will provide these future models.

We need to be wary of swallowing whole the American baby-boomer/Generation Xer rationale in the United Kingdom, but there are clearly these different styles within worship, although not necessarily divided by age alone. These values cut across the age spectrum. There are older and younger people who embrace contemporary Christianity; some might do it to Kendrick songs, others to Matt Redman but in form it is the same. I speak to people in their teens and twenties who are very happy to worship within the contemporary scene and therefore do not see what this Generation X stuff is all about. Much of the culture-specific worship taking place is actually just contemporary church to a louder beat and brighter lights, rather than strictly prospective.

Similarly, there are those teenagers and young people who find that traditional worship meets their spiritual needs and helps them to come into God's presence and live out their Christian faith each day. It is important that we recognize and affirm their place in the Church and their spirituality. In developing new forms and structures to draw in those who find the cultural gap between themselves and the Church too great to be bridged, we do not want to send the wrong signals to those who have made this step or who find that church culture amply expresses their faith.

What is the Church?

'Are you relgous?' asks one of a group of teenagers who have come round to talk about starting up a disco for younger teens. I dodge this but the conversation soon swings to the Church. It's boring... It's for old people... It's not interested in young people... We often start the debate about the Church from how we perceive it: 'It is full of older people', 'it is culturally irrelevant', 'it is not a place where young people feel they belong', 'it does or does not meet my needs', 'it is not . . . ' or 'it is . . . '.

This starting place can be used as justification to support the setting up of youth congregations or youth churches. This is a weak argument, a bit like those teenagers who come to me and say it is all right for them to sleep together because other members of the congregation are fiddling their tax or speeding etc. If something is wrong it is wrong, and it cannot be justified because something else is equally wrong.

The Church has lots of good things going for it. The young people I was chatting to about the disco were there because the Church pays a youth worker to facilitate youth initiatives. Young lives are changed and transformed even in boring traditional churches when faithful Christian people get alongside them and live out the gospel. Churches too are changed when young people get involved and use their gifts and energy for God's purposes. In my fourteen years of youth ministry some of the highest points have been seeing young people using those gifts in preaching, leading worship, teaching, sharing their faith, being the Church.

We need, therefore, to investigate whether culture-specific congregations and churches are legitimate expressions of the Church in their own right, not just in comparison with collective worship services happening elsewhere which may be viewed as culturally irrelevant. If they are not legitimate expressions, we should not be wasting time, energy and resources on them.

In the light of the above, let us look at this the other way round and ask if there is a scriptural, traditional or theological understanding that gives legitimacy to establishing culture-specific congregations and churches. To do this we essentially need to ask

'What is the Church?'

We talk about the Church in many different ways:

> 'We're going to church on Sunday'
>
> 'My church is the one next to the market'
>
> The family of the Church
>
> All-age church services
>
> Baptized into the Church

Those in our society who do not attend will usually speak of the Church in a variety of different ways. This multiple usage of the one word 'church' describes:

> the building;
>
> a meeting at that building;
>
> the people who meet at the building;
>
> what the people who meet at the building do;
>
> what the people who meet at the building are when they are not at the building.

A veritable 'house that Jack built' of confusion, misunderstanding and layered meanings. Traditionally, the Church has been defined as follows:

> The visible Church of Christ is a congregation of faithful men, in the which the pure word of God is preached, and the sacraments be duly ministered according to Christ's ordinance in all those things that of necessity are requisite of the same.[8]

We may have moved away from the idea of the Church as the building that we go to just once a week, realizing that, as the early Church had no buildings, there had to be more to the concept than that. However, the concepts of the Church that we have put in its place are equally culture-conditioned. They need to be challenged to see if they are the product of an accurate perception or equally misleading.

Ekklesia This Greek word meaning a gathering of the called, the chosen, reflects a Christianized descendant of the Aramaic term *kenishta* meaning both the whole congregation of Israel as a chosen people and also an individual gathering or synagogue. It is this idea which lies behind the usage of the term in the New Testament. We can build on this to broaden our picture of the Church as we look at further illustrations.

The Body of Christ A team with different functions and gifts working together, caring for each other, sharing in the task of building and extending the kingdom of God.

The people of God God's radical new society; a promise from Old Testament times that God would make his place among his people; he would be their God and they would be his people. The society which would result from the indwelling of God would be very different; it would practise justice and show mercy; power structures would be turned upside down; it would be a community as close as the closest family; a place where its members could discover the uniqueness of their relationship with their God.

God chooses us (John 15.16) and calls us to Christ to be his people. In a society that has been dominated by rampant individualism and is beginning to move away from it, it is important to emphasize the corporateness of being 'a chosen people'.

A spiritual house (1 Peter) A building made not of brick and timber but of living stones, being assembled not to an earthly set of blueprints but to the heavenly creator's plan. People, warts and all, are the building blocks.

The bride of Yahweh/Christ This beautiful biblical analogy or metaphor represents the devotion, purity and intimacy that God desires with his people. The Church in response is to be morally and doctrinally faithful and to seek that same loving intimacy in relationship with God that is sought in marriage.

The army of God The Church is in a battle against the forces of darkness. A liberal curate once asked me why evangelicals pray 'like there are demonic eyes peering out from behind every tree and lamp-post'. I hope not because they have been reading too much Frank Peretti, but rather, I replied, 'because they take the reality of the spiritual battle seriously'. Scripture tells us to put on our armour and be ready for the battle, 'for we wrestle not against flesh and blood but against the principalities and powers, against the spiritual hosts of wickedness in the heavenly places' (Ephesians 6.12). In most wars those who fight are men aged between 16 and 25 – the group most conspicuously missing in the Church in this country.

The vine The Church is made up of people linked to Christ and to one another, but they must also bear fruit. Those who do not bear fruit are to be pruned.

As we look at these pictures of the Church, we see ideals which are often at the centre of culture-specific worship. They are concepts that many culture-specific congregations are trying to take on board. With their search for authentic community, engagement in spiritual warfare, shared leadership etc., some of them could be closer than we might imagine to the biblical picture of the Church.

If we look more widely at Scripture, is this also true for the practical advice on the Church given in the New Testament? For example, 'Here there is no Greek or Jew, circumcised or uncircumcised, barbarian, Scythian, slave or free, but Christ is all and is in all' (Colossians 3.11); or in John 17, when Jesus prays that his disciples may be brought to complete unity. How can we have meaningful unity and diversity without it making a mockery of Christ's reconciling work on the cross? I believe the answer lies in our understanding of the word 'church' and how we use it to describe both the Church universal and the individual local church.

A question to ponder: Is the local congregation a mirror of the universal Church or is the universal Church more than the sum of the local congregations?

Obviously the universal Church, by definition, will contain people from every nation, tribe, culture, people and language. On a literal level, the local congregation is unable to replicate this, not least because it is geographically and chronologically fixed. It will be unlikely to contain representatives of the diverse Christian congregations around the world and cannot contain Christians from other centuries. So in the larger picture of Christianity down the ages all congregations are to a greater or lesser extent culture-specific. If a local congregation is therefore unable to fulfil all the criteria, does it mean that this is not what we should be aiming for? In the words of Louis MacNeice, 'There are ends which even if not reached are worth approaching.' The answer is clearly yes.

Here we come to the second important concept: culture-specific congregations are not some kind of restricted club where you have to be a certain type of person to attend. They are expressions of the Church that grow out of a community context. These expressions will be valid to others of different ages, cultures etc. Many of the services, congregations and churches around the country have older Christians who attend both to support what is happening and because they find it meets their own spiritual needs more fully.

The third dynamic is one of change, which we shall look at in more detail in Chapter 7. What happens to a culture-specific congregation as it grows older and, for example, children are born into it? There can be a broadening of the congregation profile so that it is far more representative of the range of ages, races, class etc., in the local area.

In the area in which I live and work, over 50 per cent of the town are aged under 35 but about 90 per cent of the churchgoers are aged over 35. A culture-specific congregation planted for under thirty fives is representative of the majority culture. Culture specificity does not have to be of minority cultures.

Pulling this all together, culture-specific services, congregations and churches are a legitimate form of the Church in their own right, irrespective of the failure of the mainstream Church to engage with many people's groups and cultures.

There are other aspects of the Church which impact on our thinking. To what extent do our culture-specific congregations see holiness as conformity to a set of rules, or as a by-product of a deepening relationship with God? Where do we find the unity? Unity is found at the cross, given by God and brought by the Holy Spirit:

> It is not of the nature of the Church to have a uniform form of worship, nor uniform hierarchies, nor even a uniform theology. In the light of Ephesians 4.4–6 the opposite would seem to be true. Diversity in worship; one God, one baptism and one Lord's supper – but different peoples, different communities, different languages, different rites and forms of devotion, different prayers, hymns and vestments, different styles of art and in this sense different Churches.[9]

5

Thinking it through

In Chapter 3 we identified a number of influences within the wider culture that have affected the development of culture-specific worship. Can we similarly identify influences in personal faith development which will cast light on culture-specific worship?

Faith development

Personal faith grows through a series of stages and a number of studies have looked at these; the stages are briefly summarized below. Influential faith development theories include those of Fowler, Westerhoff, Hagberg and Guelich. I will mention Westerhoff and Fowler in particular.

JOHN WESTERHOFF

Westerhoff's theory of faith development draws on the imagery of a growing tree: 'A tree in its first year is a complete and whole tree and a tree with three rings is not a better tree but only an expanded tree. In a similar way one style of faith is not better or greater than another style of faith.'[1] This growth or development of faith expands through several stages; Westerhoff describes these as follows.

Experienced faith is formulated by what people do in terms of patterns, ritual, experience, feelings of well-being, love and belonging. Explanations or the reasoning behind them are unimportant.

Affiliative faith is about identity and belonging built up from a range of experiences, including awe, ritual, identification with what is going on, that goes beyond experienced faith, because now words and the exchange of faith are important.

Searching faith is about questioning the tradition, what is passed on to you, and looking at other means of expression. It is measuring faith against experience to check out its authenticity.

Mature faith is confident about what it believes; it combines elements of both affiliative and searching faith and is able to engage confidently with a variety of views and to expect growth through these interactions.

JAMES FOWLER

James Fowler built upon the ideas of psychologists such as Eric Erickson to devise a structure around which to define his stages of faith (listed below). As faith develops we pass through a series of stages; although this is usually a progression it is also possible to step backwards and many people do not reach the latter stages. Although Fowler labels these stages differently because of his American context, what follows is the the Anglicized version, based on the report *How Faith Grows*, as reproduced in *Kaleidoscope*.[2]

Stage 0: Foundation faith (nursed faith) The beginnings of a sense of identity or self, experiences of security, love bonding, relationship formation and trust.

Stage 1: Impressionistic faith (chaotic faith or unordered faith) Moves from total dependence and imitation, begins to use stories to make sense of the world. Fact and fantasy are not distinguishable and similarly symbols are taken literally. Ritual becomes important. 'God is like my daddy.'

Stage 2: Ordering faith Becomes aware of belonging to the faith community and separates the natural from the supernatural. Anthropomorphic views of God. Takes on board the stories, practices, rituals, beliefs etc., of the faith community. 'I believe God has legs because he was walking in the garden.'

Stage 3: Conforming faith Becomes aware of others' expectations and of different conflicts and claims but tends to conform to the religious authority. Tries to understand self and the world. May not progress beyond this stage. 'My Church's beliefs are right, and I believe them.'

Stage 4: Choosing faith Takes on personal responsibility for lifestyle, beliefs and attitudes as a result of having thought through the issues for him/herself. Can express ideas in abstract terms, is willing to express own understanding against the group's. 'I think God is in favour of me being vegetarian.'

Stage 5: Balanced faith (inclusive faith or both/and faith) Feels empathy and shows active concern for all. Learns to live with contradictions and tensions, committed to own position while respecting other's. 'I hear what you are saying and think I understand where you are coming from, but cannot agree with that view.'

Stage 6: Selfless faith 'Loves life but holds it loosely, takes it seriously but not too seriously. Experiences the Kingdom of God as a reality. The most complete stage of union with God in human life. Only a few saints reach this stage.'[3] 'I have fought the good fight, I have finished the race, I have kept the Faith. Now there is in store for me the crown of righteousness' (2 Timothy 4.7–8).

A view of faith as something that passes through a series of stages is similar to psychologist Eric Erickson's scheme of the eight ages of human beings, which sees life passing through a series of stages, from basic trust – through identity – intimacy – to facing death, as a natural progression. This explains faith as something we all have, like a series of developing world-views through which we make sense of reality. Looking back on our own spiritual life we can see that it is often like a journey; we can identify different stages in that journey which are in agreement with the theorists. There is much in Christian tradition about the journey of faith and the growth and maturity of faith. However, there are a number of problems with defining faith in terms of a world-view rather than in terms of Christian belief. We are left with a range of uncertainties: Is it saying that belief is left behind as faith develops? Does the process imply that liberal faith is a higher stage than more conservative belief? Although helpful, we can find only part of the theoretical framework we are looking for in the theories of faith development.

I was talking the other day with a diocesan director of education about faith development and how people often get stuck in a childish faith even when in other areas of life and world-view they have moved on. When trouble or problems occur, this childish faith is unable to help or sustain the person but collapses again. This encourages us to look more widely for possible solutions. As well as a pyschology of faith development, we need to draw on other disciplines in order to answer some of the questions about young people, their expression of faith in worship and the changes that are taking place. Faith development theories, by themselves, do not explain why so many young people fall away from the Christian faith. To do this we need to look not just at the internal faith journey but also at its relationship with external belief, which I will call 'parent belief'. Here we can draw on some of the insights of sociology and the processes of socialization.

The key places where young people stop being active in their Christian faith are at the transition points of faith development, that is, as they move from conforming faith to choosing faith or from choosing faith to balanced faith. At these transition points there seems to be a measuring up of parent belief to see if it makes sense in the light of their new world-view. In the light of this measuring up a number of responses are possible.

Reactions to parent belief

In the same way that we can identify stages in the development of faith, we can also identify different responses to the transmission of belief to young people. This will help us decide on a possible dynamic for the passing on of belief from one generation to another. I think we can identify seven different responses by young people to parent belief. It is important to note that the phrase 'parent belief' does not just refer to the belief of Mum and Dad but rather to the overarching belief system of the Church and home in which a person is brought up.

Rejection The succeeding generation rejects the faith: they acknowledge that it was fine for their parents and obviously meaningful but it is not important in their own life. They have nothing against people being Christians and may have many positive experiences of church life. But at this stage it interferes with their own choice of morality or lifestyle.

Rebellion   They become 'anti' their parent belief Christianity: sometimes they do not just reject it as expressed by a parent but turn against every expression of the faith. This can be a product of their experience of the Church and/or of home. The outworking of this rebellion can take many forms: trying to undermine their parent belief, or intentionally taking on lifestyles and behaviour patterns to shock and offend both their parents and other contacts with the parent belief community.

Replication   They take on the outward forms of their parent belief, its religious practices, church habits etc., without taking on board the inward spiritual dimensions. This produces someone who 'knows all the answers' and who will also be very conservative about changing church practices because they feel that this is the core of their faith. This response can be at any point on the line between formal and informal traditions. It is not just in the more formal hymn-style churches that replication occurs, it also happens in churches with informal worship styles.

Resignation   They slide out of the life of faith resignedly realizing that they cannot meet its demands of lifestyle, time commitment etc. They may be living in sin or struggling with personal holiness. Or they may belong to a group that is outside faith and not have the emotional and spiritual energy, desire or support to engage in dialogue about the faith with the group; they would rather take on the values held by the group and gradually resign their allegiance to faith.

Recondition   They come to a personal faith through taking on board that part of their parent's Christian practice which they find helpful and drawing on other sources where they do not find their parent belief so helpful. This will produce a faith that fits where they are. Rather like a faithful old sofa being re-covered, the basics are left unchanged but the externals are brought up to date. The parent church might be hymns and Kendrick choruses; the reconditioned church might be Delirious and Matt Redman.

Recreation   They recreate the faith afresh, starting from first principles. Either there is no parent belief to influence the recreation or it does not count in the equation. This recreation can be into established forms and traditions and does not necessarily produce innovative forms.

Realization   They reach a point of realization that the parent belief is both real and relevant for them and embrace both its form and content. This realization can happen at a number of different life stages and not just for young people.

Like the influences on culture-specific worship that we surveyed in Chapter 3, these responses are not discrete; rather, young people's action may be a combination of responses. It is easy for parents to blame either themselves or the Church and for the Church to do likewise when young people drift away, but we do not know all the factors. The church elder who sleeps with his secretary, the family arguments, the harsh criticism or poor joke at someone's expense can all have an effect on the faith of a young person and combine with internal and external changes and pressures to affect how young people respond at these transition points.

Transition point responses

Fiona came from a 'traditional church' background. After finishing her GCSEs she decided to go to college in the nearby town; it was a time of many changes, opportunities and new experiences. She has reached a point of transition in her spiritual journey (we could describe it as a transition from synthetic to reflective faith). Would this be a point of recreation, resignation or reconditioning?

I believe it is at these transitional points that we lose people from participative Christian faith, because we still have the traditional mindset that there is one form of the Church that fits everyone, rather than acknowledging the different places that people fit in. In Fiona's case she started going with friends from college to the Evening Service at a large Anglican church with contemporary worship styles. Her new faith draws on her parent belief but is, she now feels, more up to date. We could describe this scenario as an example of reconditioned faith.

John had a different experience. He similarly went to college after his GCSEs, having previously been very involved in church life. After starting at college his appearances on Sunday started to drop off until he was rarely seen. When pressed on the subject, he talks about the pressure of work and going out on a Saturday night, and anyway he's not sure what he believes now. He still occasionally comes to church with his Mum and Dad but is no longer involved in any meaningful way.

A CASE OF RESIGNATION

These two examples are typical of many. We know that hundreds of teenagers drop out of church life each week, but faith development theories suggest that this is just part of a smooth process of growth. However, I see this as having more to do with the transitional points at which there is an opportunity to stop, reassess and question in order to make sense of faith in one's own world. At this point of reassessment, things sometimes, for whatever reason, do not add up; experientially, intellectually or psychologically people may just need the space. Whatever the reason, they drop out.

The implications of these processes for youth worship are important for both what is happening now and what will happen in the future. If our young people's starting point is within traditional worship, they will have a wide variety of options open to them at each transition point. They can rebel against parent belief and move into either contemporary or prospective faith; recreation, realization or reconditioning can result in a similar move.

This is the process that has been going on over the last twenty years, with young people moving out of traditional-style churches into contemporary-style churches. In the main this does not occur because of the proverbial stealing of sheep, although that does happen, but rather because transition points often coincide with moving away to university or to a job and instead of going to a traditional-style church young people move to one with a more contemporary style.

Having looked at those young people facing transition points within the traditional framework, what is happening to the new generation within the contemporary-style churches as they start growing through some of the faith transitions? The answer is often culture-specific worship that relates to young people where they are at, which varies from place to place and context to context. Some of this is alternative worship with a post-modern emphasis, but much is remixed contemporary worship; as Remix say, 'it's the same song but a different sound' (the organization's address is in the Appendix).

Culture-specific worship provides the same opportunity for Church-planting, mission, and evangelism for this generation that the house churches provided for the previous generation, but with differences. What these are we shall discover, but the process will involve enculturing the gospel for today, not for twenty years ago, so it will be different.

Can what we have discussed so far be put into any overall pattern? The answer is a cautious 'sort of, maybe'. I have a variety of hunches from the statistics and from experience.

Those young people from traditional churches and the less progressive contemporary churches are most likely to leave the Church completely at the transition points as they grow up. The second most likely outcome is that they will find a more lively contemporary form of worship; the third most likely is that they will remain within the particular tradition; and the least likely is that they will try a prospective service.

For those from contemporary churches, although a higher proportion are likely to remain within the Church, the most common outcome is still that they will leave the Church at the transition points. Some will look for other prospective styles of worship including the range of culture-specific services.

6

Putting it into practice

Getting started

Worship comes out of a context. We may add all the ingredients together – the latest songs, captivating video clips, state of the art lighting, drama, dance etc. – but that does not make a congregation or a church, just an event. To be a congregation there must be a community of believers. To be a church there must be a congregation that initiates, teaches, celebrates and disciples. These are the products of a context.

If it is not enough to just assemble the right bits, what are the processes for establishing a culture-specific congregation? This depends on where you are starting from and what you are aiming at.

When we launched our culture-specific service in Surrey it drew together a variety of experiences: a youth worship band that had been together for four years, the technical team that had travelled with them, the lighting and disco crew from running a monthly disco, plus dancers, drama and prayer teams of young people involved in the existing services. The net result was a service owned by the young people as well as aimed at young people.

To be successful there needs to be a pool of capital made up of the skills and experiences of those involved and opportunities as well as money. These provide a base that can be drawn on and incorporated into the service. Where there is no capital base from which to launch, then different approaches need to be taken. Think back to one of the churches I mentioned at the beginning: it had five young people in the youth group and wanted to 'do alternative worship' to get the young people in. Again I urge that this is not the way forward. The idea that merely by copying the externals of something you can produce anything of spiritual significance is a real danger. Sadly, this is why some of the new services started over the last few years have been so short-lived: the energy went into the externals rather than into the more important foundations.

If copying is not an option, what are the processes involved in forming culture-specific congregations? There are two starting points: God and young people.

We have to engage with God. What is his mission, where is he working, how has he led up to this point? To develop anything that is not anchored in this relationship with God is to 'have a form of godliness but without the power' (2 Timothy 3.5). This means spending serious time in prayer and scriptural reflection and then following this with consultation and action. This serious commitment can be demonstrated through, amongst other things, early morning prayer meetings. There is nothing like gathering at 5.30 a.m. to sort out those who are serious from those who are going along for the ride! But more seriously, when you meet every week at 5.30 a.m. for six months the result is a foundation of prayer, scriptural reflection and a unity of purpose that would not be achieved by monthly committee meetings.

There are a range of options for engaging with young people.

EVOLUTION FROM YOUTH GROUPS AND SERVICES

To begin with the young people in the youth group or fellowship. There is always a lot of scope for young people to take an active part in the mainstream services of the church, using the traditional but still effective drama, dance, readings, prayers and presentations. This input can be broadened through services by young people for the wider congregation and services with a particular youth emphasis, although we are not going to deal with these here. We are looking at something that is different in style, content, purpose and process of establishment from traditional youth worship.

If there is already a youth service in place and the young people are already identifying the difficulties they face in persuading non-Christian friends to come along, whilst being painfully aware of the culture gap between the Church and the rest of society, then the processes in stages 1 and 2 below may be worked through more quickly. As we identified in Chapter 2, evolution from a youth service has been a well-worked and successful route to the setting up of culture-specific congregations.

Stage 1: Developing a mission imperative The first thing to identify is whether the young people in the youth group have a desire to see their friends come to faith.

It is easy to get a commitment when asked 'Do you want to come to a service that isn't as boring as church but has Rave music and a video wall?' but we are not talking mere entertainment. If the young people do not have any desire to see their friends brought to faith, then further preparation work needs to be done before the journey starts. Unless the young people draw in their non-Christian friends, all any event is doing is transfering young people from one congregation to another without much growth. Not only does an expression of desire to see others come to faith provide the necessary motivation to engage with their culture, but it also mobilizes prayer alongside serious thought and reflection. After all, if something is being done for your friends, you don't want to be the one who looks stupid. It is one thing if it is the youth leader's head on the block, but another when it is yours?

Stage 2: Identifying the barriers What are the barriers to young people generally being drawn into the worshipping life of the Church?

If the group contains a mixture of Christian and non-Christian young people, then barriers can be explored together through sharing firsthand experience. Often a difference between perception and reality rears its ugly head in the process of this kind of debate. Young people may see the Church as very different from the reality. This can be put into perspective and further identified by using the experience of a few different services or events, thus earthing their worship experience in what is happening today.

These experiences are invaluable because they can dispel the illusions non-Christians have about what the Church is like, and because they also provide opportunities for the Christian young people to see things done differently and with different emphases. The great thing is that it does not matter if they like it or loathe it (so that lets us youth leaders off the hook!). The experience helps them grow in understanding of how and why things happen, what works liturgically and what doesn't. Do not forget that honest discussion of why an event or service was awful can be extremely helpful and sometimes even more constructive than a discussion of why an event was great.

Stage 3: What is worship? There needs to be reflective time in the process: time to address some of the questions about worship raised in Chapter 2, look at Scripture, work out why things are done as they are, imagine new possibilities and think through their meanings. When we set off pyrotechnics on the high altar of a fairly catholic Anglican church, we had not seriously thought through what it would mean to the older members of the church who heard about it later. It was thoughtless and inappropriate. Whereas on another occasion at a different church, using a confetti cannon in the worship was quite appropriate. No two places or situations are the same. God did not have the same plans for Peter as he had for Stephen, Paul or James. Our reflection has to be about how we worship God here, in this place, amongst these people, in ways that can be real.

Stage 4: Getting it together (1) This is the stage for drawing a group of young people and leaders together to plan, pray and prepare. When we started meeting as a group of leaders and young people to plan what became Warehouse in Guildford, there was quite a range of agendas exhibited. There was also a clear difference between the young people's concern that it would be 'too religous' or 'so naff' that it would scare off their non-Christian friends and the view of some of the leaders that it was descending into entertainment. The process of debate, listening, prayer, discussion and consultation bore fruit in an event that hit home and was effective and real.

Getting it together involves everyone floating ideas, producing potential music, slides, bits of video, logos and graphics, seeing what the computer software will do and how loud you can turn up the church PA system before the speakers fall off the pillars. Looking at possible times and venues is vital. Is it going to be a one-off special event to test the initial interest or will it happen monthly or weekly? Where will it be held? How will the time and venue flavour the event? These experiments and ideas are thrown into the melting-pot and then it is time to do it for real.

Stage 5: Planning to start This is where the group that has been through the process so far needs to take responsibility for all the different areas of activity and draw in people to help it. Culture-specific worship must have a large enough team involved in the doing. It is not and never can be a one-person show. Pete Ward once said that the Joy service was put on by its members and attended by theology undergraduates from the university coming to see what was happening. Although he spoke in jest, there is an element of truth in this; we certainly found that there were very few passengers on the organizing team at St Stephen's. The theme and framework for the worship need to be worked out in the group, then the individual teams take responsibility for different areas.

Stage 6: Holding the event There is no such thing as 'trial worship'; either something is worship or it is not, so the next stage is to do it. What, where, how often etc., is the product of the process in stages 1–5; there are no predetermined answers.

Stage 7: Assessing results It can be very hard to judge the results after just one event or service. The long-term processes and influences are the most important. Be patient, these things take time.

What if only a few of the youth group fringe came along, instead of the hordes that had been hoped and prayed for? The few that came may have thought the whole experience was fantastic and plan to bring loads of friends, or it might mean the event simply missed it and was as culturally irrelevant as Matins. Numbers are always a very bad measure of success, although if you ask any youth worker how an event went, the first thing they will say is what the attendance was like. We need to apply some kingdom values such as patience, hope and faith to our assessment: Was it worship? Was God honoured? Did it draw people into his presence? Did it challenge people to live out their Christian faith or think things through from a Christian perspective? Were lives opened up to the possibilities God offers? Did the young people on the team grow through the experience?

In practical terms this means getting the group together, asking these questions and being honest. Accept that, at the beginning, there will be bits that did not work. I remember the time when we had some creation video footage with great music and it got out of phase and played the next section of tape so that a cheery beaver ended up on screen, rather ruining the opening sequence. It is not so much the technical glitches that are important; in the first go it is more whether the overall style is correct for what you are trying to do. The learning process has to take place alongside those who attend and this makes it a humbling but building experience.

Stage 8: Getting it together (2) This is where we go back to reflection again and pick up the sequence at stage 4. At this point we need to decide whether, in the light of the experience of doing it once, the event or service is something that we should do again – modified, improved, redesigned or exactly the same as before. There is no need to try again if, after trying once, it is clear that things just will not work. Just because culture-specific worship is working in one place does not mean that it will be appropriate everywhere.

A youth worker from Southampton recounted how they started on the road to what he thought would be a service geared specifically towards young people and ended up with an all-age evening celebration. This again demonstrates the importance of not beginning with a preconceived idea or picture. Once we have set out on the road to a more participative process, the results of this process move out of our hands and new, but probably different, things become possible.

PLANTING INTO YOUTH CULTURE

Or getting started from nowhere. A number of processes for planting into youth culture exist. These include the sowing, reaping and keeping strategies described by Laurence Singlehurst; and the lifestyle of a reproducing church approach, in which the life-cycle of a church parallels that of an individual human, with stages of conception, pre-natal development, birth, infancy, adolescence, maturity and reproduction, as produced by Dr Bill Tinsley in New Zealand. Whatever our strategy, it needs to be planned, prayed, prepared, prayed, practised and prayed again.

The group of young people interested in setting up a youth disco (mentioned in the last chapter) are the early stages of a sowing/reaping/keeping strategy. They don't know it yet, but after the disco is established, and as the young people develop relationships with the youth workers, they will be invited to a Christian Rave that we shall put on. There will be Christian input into the Rave: video, video clips, DJ comments, choice of music etc., and those interested in finding out more will be able to join a small cringe-free cell group for discussion, prayer, and 'Investigating Christianity'. Out of those who become Christians within these cells will come the nucleus of a youth congregation, and out of the leadership team's cultural engagement will come the initial ideas for worship forms and styles.

STARTING FROM OUTSIDE IN YOUTH WORK

This could be as a result of detached work, schools work, coffee-bar work etc. The process is very different from those above and, in the case of relational based or detached work, the time scale is a lot longer than in the other processes. It takes about four years of contact with an external group (one that has had little or no past experience of church life) before there is any real fruit in terms of spiritual commitment.

Pete Ward lists four stages we need to work through in this process:

Before anything gets off the ground in church, we need to:

1. Get to meet young people and form friendships with them – a slow, sacrificial and time-consuming process.

2. Gain the trust of the group.

3. Learn to share our faith in terms that they can understand and relate to.

4. Start to help them develop their own authentic style of worship and praise.[1]

It is this work of building relationships and learning how to share our faith in their culture that lays the foundations for future work. This relational approach is very different from the mission approaches of yesteryear in which, once a few had made a commitment either through a schools mission or evangelistic event or by being personally brought to Christ and there were the beginnings of a potential group, the traditional process was to give them a six-week Christian basics course and then send them to the nearest church or to one where they had friends or people they knew. This model sadly works even less succesfully today than it did 10 years ago, when I remember attending a typical schools mission event in which about 60 young people made commitments and by the end of the follow-up material most had dropped out and none of them became active church members.

The alternative is to disciple and nurture young people in their culture, in ways they can relate to, and then enable them to express their faith and worship in their own culture through long-term, relationship-based discipleship strategies that have the target of producing committed Christian disciples for the long term rather than extra pew fodder in the short term. This is now being done successfully by a number of Christian youth organizations.

Discipling young people in this way is not a cop-out from challenge and commitment, nor is it saying that anything goes and we can allow heresy or anti-Christian practices in the flexibility of worship expression. But it does provide a lot more flexibility to respond to individual needs and to support, mentor and challenge.

Once we move out of traditional structures and start doing things differently or in innovative ways, the question of safety soon arises.

Safety

There is a view quite common in Christian youth work that we are becoming too concerned with safety and hence are being overprotective of our young people.[2] Whilst in real life our young people have to make major choices and decisions about their careers and their morality and choices about sex, money etc., within the life of the Church it seems that they are participating in a youth programme which often resembles Sunday School rather than youth work.

Youth worship has been a prominent exception to this dependency culture. Young people have been in positions of power and responsibility, developing not only a variety of styles of worship but also a variety of ways of organizing, planning and structuring these worship events. In the light of what happened at the Nine O'clock Service (NOS), are there genuine concerns and anxieties that we should have or are we, subconsciously perhaps, just extending the desire to keep young people dependent and stifling their gifts and ideas to keep them safe?

Let us look at some of the possible grounds for concern about youth worship, youth congregations, culture-specific and alternative worship.

THEOLOGICAL CONCERNS

The doctrines and traditions of the Christian Church protect us from heresy and error as well as being a weight for conservatism in matters of worship and cultural expression. If we let go of traditions in worship, is there also a danger that we will let go of the doctrine that defines us as Christian and slide into heresy or apostasy? If these new expressions of the Church are drifting off-line, will the leaders realize it and have the ability to do anything about it?

At first glance this is a justifiable concern, but close examination of the present scene shows that it may be unfounded. Many of the existing youth congregations are part of mainstream Churches and enjoy direct church oversight. Those that are Church plants into youth culture are predominantly linked into the Remix network which, though having a New Church emphasis, is not only strictly orthodox but also, along with New Generation Ministries, provides a variety of great resources, training events, advice and help. Icthus and Pioneer also provide spiritual oversight and support to Church plants.

The larger worship events tend to be put on by large organizations such as diocesan youth committees, national youth organizations and large churches or groups of churches, so again there is little cause for concern.

These three categories – mainstream, Church plant and larger events – make up the majority of culture-specific worship and culture-specific congregations. Of those that are left, only the real alternatives, which are trying to engage with being the Church in a post-modern society and to learn from theologians outside the mainstream Christian tradition, are in any danger of wandering off-track. Most of these are not full of teenagers but of those in their mid-twenties, thirties and forties with the theological knowledge, understanding and training to undertake the exploration. But of course it is still vitally important that there is supervision and accountability.

We need to be aware of our own motivations in any theological concern. Is there a desire that young people will worship in the way that we do and find helpful what we find helpful? Therefore we need to be aware of a possible bias in our assessment and concern.

CULT CONCERN

Television soap operas show a stream of apparently trendy Christians who are really cult leaders. How can we know if something that starts out as, or apparently is, orthodox will not develop into or already be a cult and therefore a danger? Maurice Burrell identifies certain characteristics of cults.[3] These include:

● Missionary zeal: they are very active in spreading their message and recruiting new members;

● Charismatic leadership: there is usually one dominant, powerful, charismatic leader;

● Exclusive truth: they alone have the truth; others are not only wrong but often condemned;

● Group superiority: because they alone have the truth they are not only different from but superior to those outside the group or cult;

● Strict discipline: whether this is in terms of personal prayer or fasting times, what you should wear, who you should marry, there are rules that must be kept without question;

● Repression of individuality: personal decisions are passed over to the leaders in an extreme form of shepherding;

● Doctrinal deviation: there is no room for debate; one line (usually the leader's) is sacrosanct.

Though some culture specific congregations may be zealous in evangelism, a brief glance will show that these exhibit very different characteristics from most cults. As Ben Cohen reported from the Emerging Visions Conference in York in 1995, 'there is little chance of another Chris Brain-style personality cult arising. On this week's showing the key figures appear modest and self-effacing. Overtly hierarchical and dictatorial forms of leadership are anathema to most of the scene.'[4]

There is too much desire in the alternative worship groups to escape from overbearing church structures and simple black and white answers and to create more participative, democratic ways of being the Church for it to be likely that any of them will become cults.

FEAR OF ANOTHER NOS

This is partly also what is behind the two concerns described above. I personally believe that the NOS was unique in many ways: it was the first alternative service, it had a radical agenda, it broke new ground in worship and successfully engaged with the culture. However, now that this has been done, lots of people are taking on board different aspects of the NOS vision and there is too much pooling and sharing and working with each other between alternative worship groups for one group to develop such a powerful self-identity. At the same time, the likelihood is that other Christian leaders will, through weakness and sinfulness, mistreat and abuse members of their congregations in some way. It is also a sad possibility that as the number of culture-specific congregations grows, these will occur within them. This is not a reflection on the style of worship but on fallen human nature.

THE MEDIUM

What about the medium itself? The interplay of word, picture, action and suggestion can be very powerful, but will it be giving the 'right messages'? As Simon Heathfield states:

> One of the problems of images is the high degree of sub-jectivity with which they are interpreted. This is, of course, a problem with words and text, but to a lesser degree. In a visually sophisticated age where the major-ity of younger people spend an increasing amount of time absorbing information from, and interacting with screens, it is natural to want to use the technology. However, it may well be that the images used communi-cate a completely different message than that which was in the mind of those who put them into the presentation. It also seems that people are less likely to engage critically with what they see on TV and video.[5]

If this is so, then it is not just the meanings of visual images that we should be concerned about, but the semiotics of every sermon, hymn and chorus and even the layout and architecture of our church buildings. For each contains coded messages that could be read very differently today when compared with what was in the minds of those who designed, built or preached them. This is also an area where we see the difference between modern and post-modern culture. The modernist is concerned to make sure that the right message is understood; they have already predetermined the meaning. Therefore the role of the worship service or teaching time, as they see it, is to convey that message as efficiently as possible to ensure that the participants come to the right answer. A post-modern outlook would tell the story and let people decide for themselves what it means, as individuals or as a group, allowing them to make their own connections and understandings. 'But they might get the answer wrong!' you may well say. The answer to that has to be that this is why investment in the process up until this point is the key to discipling.

THE TIME FACTOR

Culture-specific worship takes a lot of time to set up and take down and the effort is often put in by young volunteers. How can we be sure that young people are not over-burdened time-wise to the detriment of school, sleep, college, personal spiritual life etc.? This is an important concern. In employment there are severe restrictions on how many hours people can work; in health and safety there are restrictions on what equipment employees can use. In the Church, as volunteers, young people are not covered by these restrictions.

Those involved in leading and managing culture-specific worship, especially that which has evolved out of a youth service or involves young people in either setting up or operating the technical equipment, should draw up a set of practical guidelines (see the following section).

There is a tendency in church life to think 'It will never happen to us' and therefore fail to take seriously issues of safety and good practice. I would strongly encourage people to think long and seriously about safety guidelines for youth worship. Our public liability insurance contains a 'condition of care' which means taking all reasonable precautions. If we have not done so and something happens, there is the possibility of the insurers repudiating the claim.

There are a whole range of issues that we need to address concerning the safety and protection of the young people involved in running culture-specific services. These are listed in the Guidelines below, but there are other issues affecting culture-specific worship more generally that also need addressing:

- Culture-specific worship often takes place in the dark; if the power fails, are there exit lights so that people can find their way out?

- If there is a fire, are the fire exits marked and will they be illuminated if the power fails?

- Are there wires, lighting rigs or equipment obstructing the aisles and exits, etc? The local Fire Department will come to advise and help, and contacting them and heeding their advice demonstrates that we are taking all reasonable care. You may think fires in church are rare, but I was in a packed candlelit Christmas service when the organist's music caught fire. As it happened, it was an amusing mishap but it could have been much more serious.

- How accessible is the service for those with disabilities? Will they be able to make a speedy exit from the building in the event of fire or other problems?

- Numbers are another issue we need to consider. It is great to squash 300 young people into a church that seats 220, but is it sensible and is it safe?

- Similarly, are they properly supervised? What is the ratio of adults to young people? We may feel this is unnecessary in worship, but there are often visiting or spectating young people who may have other agendas or ideas. At one culture-specific service a teenage girl complained afterwards that she had been groped during the service. Those supervising can provide a watchful eye in terms of both inappropriate behaviour and pastoral need.

Culture-specific worship engages at many levels and can affect us spiritually, emotionally etc. We need to be prepared to look after those who need prayer or space or counsel or support.

GUIDELINES

Below are some of the areas that those involved in youth worship should cover in their guidelines.

Time

- What limits should we impose for each age group on the time the young people put into the setting up? This will depend on the size of the team, how often the service runs, etc.

- Will there be adequate breaks for food, etc.?

Safety

- Who can handle what technical equipment?

- How often is electrical equipment safety checked and by whom?

- If electrical equipment needs repairing, who can do it under what supervision?

- What is the insurance position in case of accident or negligence?

- What restrictions are placed on ladders and access to lighting bars, scaffold towers, etc.?

Moral issues

- How will leaders ensure that the pressure of putting on the service does not override other criteria?

- In a strong team-building situation like this, how will proper relationship distances between leaders and members be ensured?

- Will all monies be accounted for? If so, how and by whom?

- How will parental wishes be respected and acted upon?

- How will we encourage a sense of perspective in the event of success or failure?

- How will we ensure that these guidelines are followed?

Drawing up such guidelines will involve time and energy – always in short supply for leaders; but for long-term success this is essential. A number of culture-specific congregations have hit the point where the young people ask: Is it worth it? Can we be bothered? Sometimes this is true for the leaders as well. If the amount of time is not justified by the results, the whole thing grinds to a halt or it is decided to take a break or try something different. This is not such a problem for events where professional lighting and sound people are brought in or for those few Church plants and services where the equipment is already rigged.

GOOD PRACTICE

The above examples have moved us on from safety to another area of concern from a youth work perspective: good practice. Not only is what we are doing safe, is it the best approach and what are the opportunity costs of investing time and resources into the project?

Given the resources of time, energy and finance used by leaders in setting up culture-specific worship for young people, does the rest of the church youth work suffers at its expense? Many groups have found that the opposite happens. The worship draws new people into the Christian faith and its participatory nature and leadership opportunities produce new leaders from amongst the older young people and young adults, who will then strengthen the wider youth work leadership.

Do leaders get involved in culture-specific worship with young people because it is a soft option compared with other areas of youth work, or for other wrong reasons? There are a range of motivations for being involved in church youth work. Paul

Borthwick identifies two sorts of motivation.[6] First, there is the *need for achievement*. The desire to be a successful youth worker can be the product of feelings of failure in other areas of life. Youth ministry is measured in terms of how big, how successful, how many. The other motivation is the *need for affiliation*. The desire to be liked by the young people can be a result of being disliked in school. This involves spending as much time as possible with young people and success is about being accepted as one of them rather than as a discipler and enabler.

It is important not to prejudge individual cases, but there are circumstances when leaders are getting involved in culture-specific worship for a range of poor motivations. Those motivated by the need to achieve see the opportunity of big numbers, big budgets and big events. Being a church that does 'alternative worship' may at the moment be a badge of success in itself. With growing numbers of events at church, deanery and diocesan level, it is possible to be involved in one event after another.

Those motivated by the need for affiliation may see culture-specific worship as a chance to be liked and cool. Worship leaders within the Church often have the same status as rock stars outside. Leading culture-specific worship is trendy – hundreds of young people are watching you.

In both the above situations the motivations that draw people into youth ministry will attract them to culture-specific worship at the expense of the bread and butter youth ministry of nurturing, discipling and evangelizing young people. Being aware of our motivations is most of the battle in avoiding poor decisions, but good support and accountability, which we will look at later in this chapter, also help.

Are leaders working out their own dissatisfaction with worship and church structures and using the young people as both an excuse and a vehicle to do this? Some dissatisfaction is a healthy thing, encouraging change and growth, but accountability and support are important to ensure this is kept in balance.

Does culture-specific worship just pander to selfish desires for worship forms that we like and enjoy? I remember one of the first alternative services that we did in Surrey. I hated it! Everyone had worked so hard and I had really high hopes for it. There was simply something about the service which was just not me. But that was right. It was not for me. It was by the young people and for them.

Accountability and support structures

> If alternative groups . . . are to flourish in a healthy way they perhaps need to take seriously the importance of pursuing and sticking with the painful and aggravating relationship with more mainstream Churches. On the other hand I would suggest that Churches need to allow groups of younger people to experiment without imposing on them the fears, prejudices and cultural preferences of older sections of the church.[7]

If groups are allowed to set themselves up and do their own thing without supervision and accountability, it seems to be a sure-fire recipe for disaster. In practice, however, this does not always happen, because many groups take on board the need for 'integration, involvement and accountability. That means integration with the rest of the church community, the active involvement of the young because otherwise it will become irrelevant to them, and accountability to the wider church.'[8]

Different groups have addressed these needs in different ways. Groups which form a youth congregation among several other congregations within a church should find their support and accountability structures within that church or denominational structure. But there are situations where this is not so straightforward. What if those with the power feel threatened by what is happening and want to close the service down? What if it is drawing unchurched young people and church parents want something that caters more for their children? What if changes in the PCC, the churchwardens or even the incumbent produce the same desire to stop new ventures of this kind?

Sadly, all the above situations have happened to innovative youth worship initiatives and the young people have often felt hurt and rejected and lost all contact with the Church; leaders too have felt betrayed and confused. Youth work is a long-term involvement. Culture-specific worship is not a fashion accessory for the upwardly mobile church; it is about real relationships with real people. Like marriage, it should not be undertaken lightly. If culture-specific worship services move from being a series of one-off events to become more of a congregational gathering, they need to be put on a more structured basis within the wider denomination.

Where the planting of a youth congregation moves outside the parish or crosses other ecclesiastical boundaries, the following criteria may be helpful:

(a) Is there commitment to the doctrine and practice of the Church of England as expressed in the Declaration of Assent?

(b) Do the members of the planted church come from within the neighbourhood or network which the plant is designed to serve?

(c) Is there evidence of a desire to reach out to the unchurched in the defined neighbourhood or network?

(d) Do the leaders of the planted congregation display an affirming attitude to other traditions around them?

(e) Do they use authorized forms of worship, being those allowed by bishop's authority under section B of the Canons of the Church of England?

(f) Do the leaders of the congregations have episcopal ordination, licence or authorization to exercise their ministries in the local church and do those ministries include a life and teaching consonant with those normally experienced within the Church of England?

(g) Does the congregation acknowledge episcopal leadership, and accept financial and other diocesan obligations and generally participate in the common life of the diocese?[9]

This report goes on to say:

> It should be stressed that these criteria should not be used as part of an ecclesiological fundamentalism which disowns any venture that departs slightly from the norm . . . . On the other hand, notable departure in any one of these seven areas must be taken as a significant indicator that a plant is hardly serious in its claim to be part of the Church of England.

The application of these criteria to a culture-specific congregation within youth culture is not straightforward in comparison with other Church plants. However, not being straightforward is not an adequate reason to avoid wrestling with these difficult questions, for they not only put the onus on the congregation to think things through, but also ask questions about diocesan ecclesiastical structures. For example, the vast majority of full-time church youth workers are involved in some form of culture-specific worship, but there has still not yet been any national authorization for this ministry and only a handful of dioceses actually license their youth ministers.

In the event of culture-specific worship events evolving into weekly congregations, we must look again at what is and is not an authorized form of worship and how such services can be given proper authority under the Canons of the Church of England. Those who are outside the Church of England will obviously have to look carefully at similar issues with their own doctrinal and authorizing bodies.

In the case of regular events and services drawing together young people from a number of Churches and traditions, accountability needs to be placed with an overseeing body. This could be with a Council of Reference (similar to the way Youth For Christ has operated for many years) or a set of trustees (as with Holy

Disorder ministries). Alternatively the project could be overseen and accountable to the local Churches through an appropriate forum. This accountability should include not just moral and safety issues but also financial regularity and the overseeing body should act as a theological sounding-board off which ideas can be bounced and refined. In addition, a written constitution explaining the aims, objectives, accountabilities and methodology can be helpful.

On the alternative worship scene, some groups, like the Late Late Service, are concerned for 'an unhealthy copying of format rather than process'.[10] There is also a danger of transplanting wholesale practices of accountability from one group to another. There is something ironic about groups wishing to be culture-specific in worship by contextualizing and enculturing expressions of worship, if there is not a similar desire to work through the same processes for oversight and accountability. This aside, the Late Late Service's example of belonging to their local ecumenical council of Churches and their preference to 'work with other agencies rather than go it alone' are good principles to apply appropriately in other situations. The drawing up of the kind of statement of belief and purpose reproduced below is also a good principle.

As members of the Late Late Service we identify ourselves as the following:

1) Christian people united around the faith of the historical church, as expressed in its most widely accepted creeds and as revealed in the Old and New Testaments. We believe in God, we follow Jesus, and we trust in the presence and the movement of the Holy Spirit.

2) People committed to looking for and living in the realm of God (traditionally the 'Kingdom') revealed in Jesus Christ: called to love one another and to be a healing community seeking the wholeness and liberation of all people.

3) People seeking to live out and express the following beliefs:

– Each human life is a gift from God and each person has equal worth and value.

– We are called to take an active stand against any relationships, practices or structures which deny or undermine this belief.

– Human creativity is a gift from God, and a way in which we express God's image in us.

– We seek to encourage and embrace this gift in our worship and life and to enjoy and challenge contemporary culture in all its diversity.

– The resources of the earth are God's gifts to us, for which we are called to take responsibility and show care.

– We are called to live simply, identify with the poor, and know that all material possessions are gifts from God, to be shared for the common good.

The Late Late Service community is our gift to each other and to God.

So far in this chapter we have looked at authority and supervision within the mainstream of culture-specific worship, but there are groups enculturing the gospel across cultural, class, ecclesiastical and theological boundaries. In these circumstances a flexible approach may become necessary, with groups being accountable to an individual bishop. Though this of itself might create difficulties, there are circumstances when accountability to a different denomination or a New Church network with expertise in working in that culture would be a more appropriate form of supervision. This kind of flexibility goes against traditional, defensive church thinking, but it is a step towards a more network-oriented, ecumenical-based mission strategy.

There is a danger if supervision, accountability and structures become so burdensome and institutionalized that we restrict and sanitize what is happening to the extent that it loses its prophetic edge and is transformed from a movement of the Spirit to a monument, and the opportunities are lost. Balancing the creative with an accountable structure is one of the tightropes that culture-specific worship must walk.

7

What does the future hold?

Youth Congregations are a good place to start but not a
good place to end up.[1]

Changes

What does the future hold for the various forms of youth worship
and culture-specific congregations? It may be stretching too far to
imagine the scene 50 years from now, with a congregation of 70-
and 80-year-olds setting up their lighting rig for that evening's
rave worship whilst condemning younger generation's wish to
replace the chairs with pews and bring back hymns. Clearly,
although this example falters in the point it is trying to make,
things will change and for a variety of reasons.

LIFE CHANGES

We live in an ever more mobile society. People no longer have a
'job for life' and consequently members will move out of the area.
As the personnel involved in culture-specific worship change, so
the gifts – the capital base and spiritual collateral of the group –
change. Consequently the congregation will be changed.

There are other life changes that will affect the style, time and
nature of the service. As we have discovered, the arrival of children can dramatically change not just the time of a service but
also its liturgical content. What happens to the children when
they are too old to be silent partakers but young enough to want
to explore and participate in their own inimitable way? At one
alternative service there was a large wooden cross laid out on the
floor, wrapped in a wire mesh. In the opening rite members of the
congregation took a candle, lit it and stuck it into the wire mesh

around the cross, symbolizing us gathering with the cross as focus, and so on. Two 'little people' aged one and two thought this new liturgy was great and spent the service taking out the candles, blowing them out, relighting them etc. Similarly, members simply growing older will have an effect; however much people try to escape, it changes our outlook and priorities.

FAITH CHANGES

We saw in Chapter 6 how we grow through different stages of faith. As we reach each stage, we ascribe differing importance to different aspects of our spiritual and church life. That is not to say that young people and adults will necessarily grow out of culture-specific worship back into the mainstream. It might be the opposite: they may leave behind 'the individuative/reflective faith' of the mainstream and grow into a more 'conjunctive' faith[2] in the culture-specific congregation.

A friend of mine who is a priest and counsellor was recounting how those who come to him from a Christian faith often move away from faith during the counselling process, whereas those who are of no faith often embrace the Christian faith during the counselling process – a theme that a number of Christian and other counsellors have noted. Part of the reason for it is that our belief about our faith and our expression of our faith within the Christian community do not match up. Christian leaders are great at assuming that people are at one place in their spiritual development when the reality is actually very different. Examples of this can be seen right across the spectrum, from the 'Let's sing it again, this time with feeling' charismatic to the 'We're doing it my way, because I say so' liberal. We need as a Church to be much more aware of this fluidity in personal faith and belief. It is not just leading lights in national organizations who have faith crises, it is happening in many of our churches. People's faith may have changed on the inside but the external expression has usually remained the same.

Smaller, more flexible youth or culture-specific congregations are, at present, able to adapt and change. They often have the openness to engage with people at a deeper level, to be more person-oriented than organization-centred. Thus they can change where there is the theological freedom to do so. In other words, the more adaptable culture-specific congregations have the potential to change as a direct result of the faith change of their individual members. The direction of this change, however, is completely unknowable in advance. Whether we can hazard some guesses or not is a very good question. How fast the process of institutionalization will progress within culture-specific congregations also remains to be seen.

CULTURE CHANGES

Who can predict the vagaries of popular culture? As I write this there is a Spice Girls boom. When you read it, it will (I hope!) be over. There are, however, deeper changes affecting the culture such as further transition into post-modernity and post-post-modernism and the decline of modernism and rationalism; the rise in apocalyptic culture as we approach the millennium and the post-millennial effects the other side of it; and the impact of technology and political values on culture. All are unquantifiable in advance but could affect what happens in the future in a major way.

MAINSTREAM CHURCH CHANGES

'Jesus Christ the same yesterday, today and forever', chiselled in stone over the door, can give the impression that the Church never changes. And many would agree. But it is not just in recent years that expressions of the Church have altered dramatically.

Over the last millennium, buildings have seen many changes. Screens have come, gone, returned and gone again. Pews have done the same: when the 'weakest went to the wall', churches had no furniture and those who could not stand found a bench seat at the edge; now we are returning to flexible open spaces. Icons and statues have come, gone, and are returning. Music was in the hands of the many in the minstrels' gallery, in the hands of the one with the rise of the organ, back to the many with the music group, and now sometimes with the one again, accompanied by keyboard, sequencer, midi and DAT recordings. Liturgy has similarly undergone development: Latin to vernacular to Series 1, 2 and 3 to ASB to *Patterns for Worship* to new Prayer Books. We have also seen the family service movement, the parish communion movement, the charismatic movement, the all-age movement, the alternative worship movement. Alongside these have been the changes in theological emphasis.

The Church has always taken into the mainstream that which has been successfully pioneered on the fringes, although there is usually a time gap of sufficient length in this process to ensure that it will be out of date with the wider culture by the time it has been taken on board. None the less it does mean that, even if it is sometimes difficult to see, change does happen and is happening in the wider Church. There are also elements within the mainstream Church which do not change and tradition can be a protection against false doctrine.

Tradition is also rich in spiritual capital. One of the problems for culture-specific congregations is often where to draw this spiritual capital from. As Andy Thornton muses on the Internet: 'Alternative worship might be the refuge of the post-evangelical (or whatever name you choose for that experience) who bring with them a mighty wealth of spiritual collateral from their lifetime's experience, but not a place where they necessarily accrue more.' This does not mean, however, that alternative worship or culture-specific congregations can be seen as nothing more than a passing phase, even if they do in fact 'pass'.

The future

The future of culture-specific worship and congregations will be determined by many factors and it is just as difficult to speculate about what might happen in the future as it is to define their nature in the present. We can begin by looking at their future in terms of a combination of the following: absorption, adaptation and evolution.

ABSORPTION

> What is happening in youth groups today is what will be happening in the Church in twenty years' time. (Pete Ward)

Over time, the mainstream Church culture will absorb some elements of what is happening in today's culture-specific worship services. This has proved to be the case with earlier innovations and renewals, most recently the way in which the 'chorus culture' of Christian youth work 30 years ago has been absorbed into the mainstream of Christian worship today. Our main services and congregational structures will similarly absorb some of the key features of today's culture-specific worship. This might be seen practically as a greater emphasis on visual imagery and less emphasis on the written word. Where liturgy is used, it may involve more movement, the senses of taste, touch and perhaps smell, and services other than the eucharist. Some of the technical developments may become as commonplace as the printing press made hymn books.

The speed and extent of this process of absorption will obviously differ from one congregation to another, and the content of what is accepted and rejected will also vary. As in churches today, some congregations will worship in more modern ways than others; some will prefer worship that stands at one stage along the 'absorption line', whilst others are happier further on or further back. Maybe some of the young people of the future will joke about churches who are still doing choruses with guitar or choruses at all! Whether this absorption will mean a move back towards single-congregation worship centres, like the church buildings we have had up until comparatively recently, or whether we will remain multi-congregational, will depend on how some ideas, influences and practical expressions of community from the culture-specific congregations are taken on board.

For example, we saw earlier the involvement of a search for value, belonging and community, as well as participation and self-expression, in the dynamic leading to culture-specific congregations. These elements are more difficult to absorb into

101

mainstream Church culture than some of the external expressions, because they affect the structure, nature and power relationships within congregations. They challenge the very heart of mainstream institutional Church.

ADAPTATION

If absorption is the process of change from culture-specific worship to the dominant mainstream culture, then adaptation is the process of change within the culture-specific congregation. This change will have external as well as internal dynamics. It does not take long to make traditions and patterns the established norm and the same is also true of the leadership structures and personnel. When this happens, the power relationships change, lose the original fluidity and spontaneity and become institutionalized: a man, a movement, a monument. It is always sad when a church gets stuck at a certain point, does not move on and finds itself repeating last year's programme because that was what they always did. It ends up like the church that was using the temporary service sheets twenty years later.

The internal pressures towards change may come from members growing older, or changes in their life situations and their faith. It may also come from the need to discuss certain issues such as children in worship and their involvement in the community as the number of members with families increases. It is one thing to be part of a rave congregation which meets from 10 p.m. until 1 a.m. when you are 25 and single, but a very different matter when you are 30, the children are waking or needing to be fed in the night and you have to be up at 6 a.m. every day.

Situations change and expectations, needs and outlooks change with them. This is already the case with Soul Survivor in Watford, which now holds a morning as well as evening service each week. The morning service, geared to families and those with children, still retains the emphasis on intimate worship, relationship and evangelism that is the ethos of the evening worship. One of the spin-offs that has come sooner than many expected has been the need to develop work with children and there are plans for mums and tots groups and after-school children's clubs. Soul Survivor will not be the only youth congregation to adapt in this way, keeping their primary mission to the non-Christian young people in their area (some 98 per cent of the 25,000 teenagers in Watford) while also ministering to those with children who identify Soul Survivor as their church.

This type of pressure on the culture-specific congregation will mean that it will have to adapt its structures for long-term survival. The spiritual collateral which comes with congregational members will be a significant tool and influence in determining the extent and conduct of this process of change.

EVOLUTION

The third option for change is that the culture-specific congregation will evolve as and when it needs to, tending more towards regular change.

As culture changes, an adaptation of some form will take place as a reaction. Either there will have to be a constantly varying membership or those involved will have to become cultural chameleons, adapting in response to changes and developments as and when they are encountered. An element of this can be seen in the way that some of the house churches have reinvented themselves as 'alternative'.

Evolution offers a positive alternative to stagnation, institutionalization and the road which eventually leads to cultural irrelevancy. It does, however, also carry with it the danger of always mimicking the mainstream secular culture – usually one step behind, which was one of the hallmarks of naff Christian music in the 1970s and 1980s.

As well as development by a combination of evolution, adaptation and absorption there are other possibilities.

DEATH

Some culture-specific congregations will inevitably cease to be. Over the two years it has taken to research and write this book a number of congregations and services have ceased to meet; others have reinvented themselves or changed direction dramatically. If we looked upon the setting up of a youth service or congregation as a piece of participatory, peer-led youth work then this would be a familiar outcome.

In a different youth work setting, the project might be a bus or a skateboard facility or a go-cart building. A group of young people come together round a project; it works for them, they grow up and move on and the succeeding generation wants to do something different. It is futile to expect the next generation to want to do a go-cart project as well. However, we often assume that because it is about God and because it is successful for one generation, we cannot let it die. We can. This does not deny the spiritual reality of what God did with the group; the reality will show itself over the years ahead in their Christian lives.

TAKEOVER

The influences that we identified in chapters 3 and 5 do not only apply to young people. There are adults in many congregations who feel growing dissatisfaction with the Church. A youth congregation or other culture-specific congregation can gradually be taken over as an opportunity for adult dissatisfactions to be addressed and the young people are slowly squeezed out. This had happened at a couple of culture-specific congregations I contacted; the adults' desire for more 'charismatic worship' and 'times of ministry' than were permitted in the mainstream services had first reduced the youth emphasis and then reduced the youth. This is one of the reasons why proper supervision and accountability are so important.

DISASTER

Coming to a natural end is all well and good, but it is important that culture-specific congregations do not come to a premature end through disaster. As we have seen with the NOS, and our look at safety in Chapter 6, there is the potential to go off-track in many areas. Good accountability and supervision can help reduce this, but people are fallen, they make mistakes and sometimes deliberately do wrong. We can therefore expect some culture-specific congregations to end in breakup, misunderstanding and hurt, even if this is not splashed across the pages of the national newspapers. It is important that when this happens we are prepared as the Church to pick up the pieces, bind up the hurt and learn from the mistakes.

Why be concerned?

Why should we be concerned about what the future may hold for culture-specific congregations? Does this say more about our own concerns and anxieties than a desire to see where God may be leading his church?

One of the motivations for church youth work is that of passing the faith on to the next generation – sometimes without giving them space to discover some of it for themselves. This can also be seen in our worship. Our obvious hope and desire is that the next generation will experience God and therefore want to worship him, but often it is difficult for us to envisage them doing this in ways other than those that we have found helpful. This is partly what is behind the immense effort, in time and money, which goes into the socializing of young people into church culture.

The problem is that what may be liberating for one person is sometimes a restriction or encumbrance for another, particularly when that other person is of another generation and culture. Beautiful classical music may lift one person into the presence of God while another finds it less helpful. How does this affect our concern for the future? Simply, that if we believe that culture-specific worship is a temporary stage that young people 'go through'

before returning to proper/traditional/charismatic/Catholic/
rational (delete as appropriate) worship, we shall be disappointed
when this is not the result.

It is already very apparent that culture-specific congregations are
producing a range of gifted and talented young leaders who are
able to work in teams and use and develop one another's gifts.
They are innovative in designing, planning and staging worship
which can engage with the culture and reflect theologically on
the issues it raises. These will be the natural leaders of the Church
in this country tomorrow, as well as the leaders of today's local
church. So far from returning to 'proper' church, they will be
leading us on into new and different places.

It could be that out of these post-modern expressions of the
Church, youth congregations and culture-specific services are
growing new ways of 'being' and 'doing' the Church that will
challenge and transform as Columba or Luther did. The traditional Church is slowly bleeding to death and much of the
contemporary Church is partying on the *Titanic* of modernism. If
the Church is to have any relevance in the next millenium except
as a host for the *Antiques Road Show* it needs to take hold of these
emerging visions.

Appendix
Help file

Organizations

Be Real, Internet home page   http://www.maths.nott.ac.uk

Church of England National Youth Office   Tel: 0171 222 9011
Fax: 0171 233 1094

(Peter Ball and Maxine Green)
Church House
Great Smith Street
London
SW1P 3NZ

Church Pastoral Aid Society   Tel: 01926 334242
Athena Drive   e-mail: sales@cpas.org.uk
Tachbrook Park   Web site:
Warwickshire   http://www.cpas.org.uk
CV34 6NG

Genesis Arts Trust   Tel: 0171 240 6980
6 Broad Court
London
WC2B 5QZ

Greenbelt   http://www.greenbelt.org.uk

Holy Disorder   Tel: 01684 293233
(Peter Sibely)
49 Barton Street
Tewkesbury
GL20 5PU

Late Late Service
PO Box 176
Glasgow
G4 9ER

http://www.greenbelt.org.
uk/altqrps/usbeliv.html

New Generation Ministries
Severn Ridge
29 Gloucester Road
Almondsbury
Bristol
BS12 4HH

Tel: 01454 625577
e-mail: NGM@NGM/uk.org

Oxford Youth Works
The Old Mission Hall
57b St Clements
Oxford
OX4 1AG

Tel: 01865 438383

Remix
PO Box 58
Chichester
West Sussex
PO19 2UD

Tel: 01243 531898
Fax: 01243 531959

Soul Survivor
7 Greycaine Road
Watford
Herts
WD2 4JP

Tel: 01923 801801

Recommended books

Simon Heathfield, *DIY Worship: Enabling Young People to Respond to God in Everything*, CPAS, 1996

Resource pack of over 200 worship ideas and practical considerations for work with younger teens and others, complete with CD of 11 music tracks and text and graphics for PC.

Bob Mayo, *Gospel Exploded*, Triangle, SPCK, 1996

A hands-on account of a culture-specific congregation for 'pre-non-Christian' young people in South London – the problems and the possibilities.

Roland Howard, *The Rise and Fall of the Nine O'clock Service*, Mowbray, 1996

A useful look inside the goings on at the NOS.

Pete Ward, *Worship and Youth Culture*, Marshall Pickering, 1993

Theory and practical ideas based on the experience of Oxford Youth Works' Joy service in 1991 and 1992.

Bibliography

Ball, Peter, 'Growth or dependency. Polarity of youth work practice' in Pete Ward (ed.), *Relational Youth Work*, Lynx, 1995.

Borthwick, Paul, *Feeding Your Forgotten Soul*, Zondervan, 1990.

Breaking New Ground. Church Planting in the Church of England, Church House Publishing, 1994.

Burrell, Maurice, *The Challenge of the Cults*, IVP, 1981.

Carey, George, *Spiritual Journey. The Archbishop of Canterbury's Pilgrimage to Taizé with Young People*, Mowbray, 1994.

Frank, Penny, *et al.*, 'God, me and you', *CY*, CPAS, September 1996.

Gerali, Steve, *The Church and Youth Ministry*, Lynx, 1995.

Green, Laurie, *Let's Do Theology*, Mowbray, 1990.

How Faith Grows: Faith Development and Christian Education, National Society/Church House Publishing, 1991.

Howard, Roland, *The Rise and Fall of the Nine O'clock Service*, Mowbray, 1996.

In Tune with Heaven. The Report of the Archbishop's Commission on Church Music, Hodder & Stoughton, 1992.

Lent, Holy Week, Easter, Church House Publishing/Cambridge University Press/SPCK, 1986.

Mayo, Bob, *Gospel Exploded*, SPCK, 1996.

Tomlinson, D., *The Post Evangelical*, SPCK/Triangle, 1995.

Ward, Pete, *Worship and Youth Culture*, Marshall Pickering, 1993.

Ward, Pete, *Growing Up Evangelical*, SPCK, 1996.

Westerhoff, John, *Will our Children Have Faith?* Harper & Rowe, 1976.

Youth A Part, Church House Publishing, 1996.

Notes

Introduction

1. *Mixmag*, 54, November 1995.

1 Something is happening in youth worship

1. *Youth A Part*, Church House Publishing, 1996, p. 27.
2. *Coventry Diocesan Directory 1997*, insert p. 6
3. Bob Mayo, *Gospel Exploded*, SPCK, 1996.
4. See Pete Ward, *Growing Up Evangelical*, SPCK, 1996, p. 214.
5. *Youth A Part*, p. 68.
6. Ian Savoury, Director of Norwich Youth For Christ.

2 Dry ice and laser beams

1. *Monocle* magazine, 1991.
2. Louise, aged 18, Woking Holy Disorder.
3. Dr Paul Roberts, 'Liturgy and mission in postmodern culture: some reflections arising from "alternative" services and communities', unpublished paper from the Lambeth New Worship Day, 1995.
4. *Lent, Holy Week, Easter*, Church House Publishing/Cambridge University Press/SPCK, 1986, p. 187.
5. *Mixmag*, 1995.
6. George Carey, *Spiritual Journey. The Archbishop of Canterbury's Pilgrimage to Taizé with Young People*, Mowbray, 1994.
7. Gianfranco Tellini, *Symbols, Worship and the Word*.
8. Natasha, aged 23, Lifetime Service, Worcester.
9. Alison, aged 21.
10. NOS member, aged 15. Roland Howard, *The Rise and Fall of the Nine O'clock Service*, Mowbray, 1996.

11. Natasha, Worcester.

12. Louise, Woking.

13. Peter Ball, 'Growth or dependency. Polarity of youth work practice' in Pete Ward (ed.), *Relational Youth Work*, Lynx, 1995, p. 82 (slightly adapted).

14. *In Tune with Heaven. The Report of the Archbishop's Commission on Church Music*, Hodder & Stoughton, 1992, p. 80.

15. Lord Runcie, *Sunday Telegraph*, 9 February 1997.

16. William Temple.

3 Getting behind the scenes

1. See Leslie J. Francis and William K. Kay, *Teenage Religion and Values*, Gracewing, 1995, and Peter Brierley, *Reaching and Keeping Teenagers*, MARC, 1993.

2. Pete Ward, *Youthwork* magazine, April 1993.

3. Roberts, 'Liturgy and mission in postmodern culture'.

4. Nigel McCullough, opening address at Eagles' Wings 1994.

5. Steve Chalke, *Youthwork* magazine, April/May 1993.

6. David Johnson and Jeff Van Vonderen, *The Subtle Power of Spiritual Abuse*, 1996.

7. Penny Frank, *Discussion at Dick Farr's Place*, CPAS, 1996, summarized as 'God, me and you' in *CY* magazine, September 1996.

8. Roberts, 'Liturgy and mission in postmodern culture'.

9. Gustav Gutierrez, *A Theology of Liberation*, SCM, 1985, p. 307.

10. Laurie Green, *Doing Theology*, Mowbray, 1990.

11. Pete Ward, *Worship and Youth Culture*, Marshall Pickering, 1993, p. 37.

12. Laurie Green. *Let's Do Theology*, Aston Training Scheme, 1988.

13. Sarah Maitland, *Church Times*, 10 May 1996.

14. Ibid.

15. Howard, *The Rise and Fall of the Nine O'clock Service*.

16. Be Real, Internet home page.

17. *The Iona Community Worship Book*, Wild Goose Publications, 1991.

18. Be Real, Internet home page.

19. 'I need you to hold me', by Brenda LeFave, Mercy Publishing/Thank You Music, 1991.

20. 'The culture which often prevails in our congregations is one which socialises adults into perpetual childhood.' J. M. Hull, *What Prevents Christian Adults from Learning*, SCM, 1985, p. 7.

21. D. Tomlinson, *The Post Evangelical*, SPCK/Triangle, 1995, p. 75.

22. Richard Eckersley, 'Failing a generation: the impact of culture on the health and well-being of youth', paper presented to the Australian Rotary Health Research Fund's Fifth International Conference, November 1992.

23. *Mixmag.*

24. George Carey, Archbishop of Canterbury, at a meeting of the Full-Time Youth Workers Association, 7 November 1996.

4 What is worship? What is the Church?

1. *Ishmael's Family Worship*, Kingsway, 1988, no. 44.

2. Penny Frank, *Discussion at Dick Farr's Place*, CPAS, 1996.

3. Exodus 3.14.

4. Ephesians 2.13 (RSV).

5. *Sunday Telegraph*, 19 July 1992.

6. Steve Gerali, 'Paradigms in the contemporary Church that reflect generational values', in *The Church and Youth Ministry*, Lynx, 1995, p. 59.

7. Ibid.

8. Article 19, Thirty-nine Articles, *The Book of Common Prayer*, 1662.

9. Hans Küng.

5 Thinking it through

1. John Westerhoff, *Will our Children Have Faith?*, Harper & Rowe, 1976.

2. Anglican report edited by J. Astley, *How Faith Grows: Faith Development and Christian Education*, National Society/ Church House Publishing, 1991; reproduced in *Kaleidoscope*, NCEC, 1993.

3. Ibid.

6 Putting it into practice

1. Ward, *Worship and Youth Culture*, p. 17.

2. Ward, *Growing Up Evangelical*.

3. Maurice Burrell, *The Challenge of the Cults*, IVP, 1981 (adapted).

4. Ben Cohen, 'Boldly going but where to?', *Church Times*.

5. Simon Heathfield, 'No alternative – issues of young people and worship', unpublished paper, 1996.

6. Based on Paul Borthwick, *Feeding Your Forgotten Soul*, Zondervan, 1990, pp. 23–4.

7. Dave Tomlinson, 'Rave on', *Church of England Newspaper*, 1 September, 1995.

8. Wendy Beech, *Young People Now*, November 1995.

9. Report, *Breaking New Ground. Church Planting in the Church of England*, Church House Publishing, 1994, pp. 32, 33 (slightly adapted).

10. Rachel Morley, formerly of the Late Late Service.

7 What does the future hold?

1. J. Sertin, 'Worship, youth and the Church', paper given at discussion day, Norwich, 1996.

2. Fowler is quoted in Astley (ed.), *How Faith Grows*.